2004 POET...

ONCE UPON A RHYME

IMAGINATION FOR A NEW GENERATION

South Yorkshire

Edited by Lynsey Hawkins

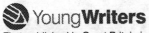 Young**Writers**

First published in Great Britain in 2004 by:
Young Writers
Remus House
Coltsfoot Drive
Peterborough
PE2 9JX
Telephone: 01733 890066
Website: www.youngwriters.co.uk

SB ISBN 1 84460 446 2

Foreword

Young Writers was established in 1991 and has been passionately devoted to the promotion of reading and writing in children and young adults ever since. The quest continues today. Young Writers remains as committed to engendering the fostering of burgeoning poetic and literary talent as ever.

This year's Young Writers competition has proven as vibrant and dynamic as ever and we are delighted to present a showcase of the best poetry from across the UK. Each poem has been carefully selected from a wealth of *Once Upon A Rhyme* entries before ultimately being published in this, our twelfth primary school poetry series.

Once again, we have been supremely impressed by the overall high quality of the entries we have received. The imagination, energy and creativity which has gone into each young writer's entry made choosing the best poems a challenging and often difficult but ultimately hugely rewarding task - the general high standard of the work submitted amply vindicating this opportunity to bring their poetry to a larger appreciative audience.

We sincerely hope you are pleased with our final selection and that you will enjoy *Once Upon A Rhyme South Yorkshire* for many years to come.

Contents

Brampton Ellis CE Junior School

Emma Simpson (10)	15
Abbie Pattison (10)	15
Daniel Howell (10)	15
Christopher Rigby (11)	16
Leigh Marrow (10)	16
Josh Evers (10)	16
Amy Graham (11)	17
Josh Moore (11)	17
Dillon Harris (11)	17
Charissa Leigh Garner (10)	18
Thomas Lelliott (11)	18
Natalie Vardy (11)	19
Ryan Jackson (11)	19
Luke Johnson (11)	20
Jordan Wood (10)	20
Luke Theaker (10)	20
Laura Clarkson (10)	21
Rebecca Brown (11)	21
Josh Caddick (10)	22
Brooke Gale (10)	22
Oliver Banks (11)	22

Dinnington Primary School

Laura Jean Keetley (11)	23
Hannah Gregory (11)	24
Thomas Perrie (10)	24
Neil Fletcher (10)	25
Jacob Robinson (10)	25
Simon Wagstaff (11)	26
Kyle Downs (11)	26
Rebecca Page (10)	27
Rhian Richardson (10)	27
Alex Keeton (10)	28
Emily Skill (11)	28
Barbara Maia (11)	28
Chloe Hamilton (10)	29
Ashley Johnson (10)	29
Ashley Wilde (11)	30
Jake Whitworth (10)	30
Nathan Gregory (9)	31

Lewis Dabell (11)	48
Gabrielle Bousfield (11)	48
Kara Hall (10)	49
Faye Miller (11)	49
Hollie Chapman (8)	50
Samantha Sanderson (10)	50
Emma Townend (9)	51
Corey Butler (11)	51
Jade Ratcliffe (10)	52
Matthew Quinn (10)	52

Grenoside Community Primary School

Rebecca Toone (10)	53
Abigail Ruston (10)	54
Harry Davison (10)	54
Della Newton (10)	55
Matthew Phipps (10)	55
Jessica Brennan (10)	56
Brady Edwards (10)	56
Rachel Hurst (9)	57
Laura L A Harrison (10)	58
Chelsey Deighton (10)	58
Natalie Bamforth (10)	59
Greg Marshall (10)	59
Lydia Beaumont (10)	60
Kaylee Beth Hardy (10)	60
Harry Rosewarne (10)	61
Ryan Marritt (10)	61
Larni Baverstock (10)	62
Rebecca Holmes (10)	62
Alex Livett (10)	63
Joe Scholey (11)	63
Lauren Bilby (10)	64
Benjamin Gregory (10)	65

Hucklow Primary School

Carissa Louise Shaibi-uter (10)	65
Lewis Barry (10)	66
Trelawny Brown (10)	66
Amy Louise Farrell (9)	66
Jahed Ahmed (10)	67

Ashleigh Crump (11)	67
Kyle Peachey (10)	67
Saeed Yusuf (11)	68
Bilal Qasim (9)	68
Shelina Khan (10)	69
Aneesa Ahmad (9)	70
Manal Al-Hakam (11)	70
Natalie Ardron (10)	71
Kyle Judge (10)	71
Joseph Luke Grimwood (10)	72
Amir Munir (9)	72
Micah Slater-Clayton (10)	72
Sidrha Ali (10)	73
Bradie Modest (10)	73
Ali Alabbasi (9)	73
Thomas Paredes-Lee (9)	74
Conal Khan (10)	74
Aaron Greenwood (10)	74
Olivia Stead (10)	75
Munief Mukerker (10)	75
Shumina Khan (9)	75
Zain Mohammed (10)	76
Kayleigh Ann License (10)	76
Rowan Chalmers (10)	77
Marvis Campbell (10)	77
Abdulrahim Elhmayle (10)	78
Jordan Fearnley (11)	78
Hassan Ramzan (11)	79
Khalid Sahal (11)	79
Grant Priestley (10)	79
Victoria Billam-Thorp (11)	80
Daniel Hancock (11)	81

Nether Green Junior School

Emma Broadhead (10)	81
Imogen Cassels (7)	82
Hannah Slaughter (9) & Caroline Barton (10)	82
Lucy Bradley (8)	83
David Cousins (8) & Jennifer Cousins (11)	83
Elliot Whiteside (8)	84
Holly Williams (10)	84

Maddy Cousins (10)	85
Eigen Horsfield (10)	85
Sam Denton (9)	86
Laura Lee (10)	86
Grace Hector (11)	87
Tessa Godley (10)	87
Pouyan Maleki (9)	87
Serafina Body (8)	88
Isobel Stocker (10)	88
Stephanie Broomhead (8)	89
Hannah Bateman (8)	89

Owston Park Primary School

Aaron Messen (11)	90
Matthias Paul Lambert (11)	90
Adam Blackburn (11)	91
Laura Purdy (10)	91
Adam Thorpe (10)	92
Thomas Johnson (11)	93
Lauren Winfield (11)	93
Lorna White (11)	94

Rudston Preparatory School

Jamie Barrett (9)	94
Thomas Velamail (9)	95
Nabeel Ahmed (9)	95
Joshua Jackson (8)	96
Lydia Sharpe (8)	96
Anastasia Efthymiou (8)	97
Brydie Adams (8)	97
Amy Croggon (9)	98
Nour Assous (8)	98
Alice Jones (8)	99
Oliver Dennis (9)	99
Bradley Cutts (9)	100
George Daly (9)	100
Thomas Henderson (9)	101

Thurgoland CE Primary School

Sarra Murphy (11)	101
Hayley Hewitt (10)	101
Matthew Waterhouse (11)	102
Simon Rodley (10)	102
Greg Holmes (10)	103
Gabbi St Matthew-Daniel (10)	103
Alice Dodd (10)	104
Adam Dewsnap (11)	104
Bethany Dobbin (11)	105
Hannah Newbery (11)	106
Joey Brayford (11)	107

Tickhill St Mary's CE Primary & Nursery School

Rhys Kyte (11)	108
Michael Hunter (10)	108
Tui Krösschell (10)	109
Georgia Ashton (10)	109
Holly Parker (11)	110
Emily Sidebottom (9)	111
Rebecca Wells (11)	111
Peter Evison (10)	112
Eliza Harman (8)	112
Daniel Donnelly (10)	113
Ben Carter (10)	113
Josiah Brown (10)	114
Stephanie Clark (10)	114
Joshua Oldham (10)	115
Holly Jackson (8)	115
Georgiana Oldham (8)	116
Zack Levers (9)	116
Natasha Jewison (10)	117
Zoe Walters (11)	117
Matthew Day (10)	118
Jodie Leigh Hide (7)	118
Christopher Marsden (8)	119
Tahla Krösschell (7)	119
Kirsty Marsden (10)	119
Leah Brown (9)	120
John Baines (8)	120

Tessa Allen (10)   121
Joanne Verity (11)   121
Abigail Ametewee (10)   122
Andrew Cotton (10)   122
Francesca Hopkin (7)   123

Toll Bar Primary School
Thomas Fritchley (7)   123
Gavin Frost (11)   123
Elizabeth Taylor (11)   124
Katie Robinson (10)   124
Chelsea Fletcher (11)   125
Samuel Danby (11)   125
Jessica Job (8)   126
Faran Hamblett (7)   126
Laura Nicholas (6)   127
Nicky Harvey (8)   127
Jade Ball (8)   127
Jade Deere (10)   128
Tom Chudley (8)   128
Danielle Caudwell (8)   129
Nathan Didcott (8)   129
Lauren Butler (11)   129
Declan Fluin (6)   130
Martin Crosby (11)   130
Charlotte Bacon (7)   131

Wath Central Junior School
Harry Woodward (7)   131
Matthew Leyland (10)   131
Megan Rees (9)   132
Jasmin Oxer (9)   132
Sam Drury (10)   133
Matthew Elliss (9)   133
Jack Hobson (9)   134
Victoria Hammond (10)   134
Holly Fisher (10)   135
William Campbell (9)   135
Jake Blunt (9)   136
Katie Johnson (10)   136

Hannah Mattingley (7)	137
Chloe Williams (8)	137
Ellie Mae Wood (8)	138
Luke Newman (7)	138
Alex Levitt (7)	138
Chloe Edwards (7)	139
Emily Fisher (7)	139
Hannah Moore (8)	139
Daniel Howell (8)	140
Jack Smith (10)	140
Shay Murray (8)	140
Sarah Robertshaw (10)	141
Jade Newell (9)	141
Dominic Jones (10)	142
Emily Beaumont (10)	142
Freya Hewett (7)	142
Hollie Smith (9)	143
Rachael Duke (8)	143
Keeley Newell (9)	144
Alice Woodcock (9)	145
Ruth Rocha Lawrence (10)	146
Ashley Sturman (10)	146
Thomas Andrews (10)	147
Laura Lois Maskrey (10)	147
Aaron Gwatkin (9)	148
Thomas Hammond (9)	148
Lewis Lowe (8)	149
Kimberley Frodsham (9)	149
Shannon Skelton (7)	149
Amy White (8)	150
Sophie Kirkham (9)	150
Lucy Hardwick (8)	151
Joshua Robinson & Megan Moffatt (9)	151
Georgia Sanders (9)	151
Casey Amanda Moule (9)	152
Kane Tasker (9)	152
Sophie Duggan (8)	152
Lorna Joan Theaker (8)	153
Helena Leather (7)	153
Joseph Elliss (7)	153
Alexander Ng (8)	154

The Poems

Peter Buys Pop

Peter went to the shop.
He drank some poisonous pop.
He spilt some on his top.
Oh dear, what a flop.

He went back to the shop
To buy a mop.
On his way he had a flop.
A policeman cried, 'Stop!'

I saw Peter chasing the mop.
A car ran him over, it didn't stop.
He got up and had to hop.
Two more cars came, they didn't stop.

Poor Peter was in a flop.
He had lost his mop
And his pop.
Goodbye to Peter, what a shock!

Sarah Siddall, Akeeb Hussain & Adam Taylor
Abbey School (For children with moderate learning difficulties)

Clouds

I hover over different countries,
Sometimes I am taken over by the blue sky,
I turn a murky grey when I am poorly,
I spit all over the world,
Spreading rapidly across the sky,
With my cotton wool hug I touch the angels,
I watch the birds pass by,
As other people watch me
Pull faces in the sky.

Eve Cantrill (10)
Abbey Lane Primary School

When You Haven't Got A Home

When you haven't got a home it's like music without a note,
No one wants you, no one wants to listen to you,
It's like being invisible,
No one sees you or pays attention to you.
When you cry, there's no shoulder to cry on.
When you are hungry, there's no food to eat.
When you smile, no one smiles at you, or with you.
When tears stream down your eyes
And it feels like someone's turned a tap on inside you,
There's no tissue to wipe them with.

When you haven't got a home it's like a snail without a shell,
There's nowhere to hide,
Nowhere to curl up.

When you haven't got a home
It's like you've been thrown into a danger zone,
Something terrible could happen any second.
It feels like you're a piece of rubbish someone's just thrown away,
It feels like life's not worth living.
If you hadn't got a home, how would you feel?

Lauren Bajin-Stone (11)
Abbey Lane Primary School

Smoke

I can sneak through the smallest gaps.
I hide the biggest things.
I'm as stealthy as a spy.
I can kill you when I reach for your lungs.
To fabric I can give a horrible scent.
My finger can sting your eyes.
My body can be swirled by the wind.

Zac Grainger (10)
Abbey Lane Primary School

Volcano

I'm as tall as a skyscraper
But I have sorrow inside me.
My anger is too much,
My insides come oozing out,
Shooting as far as the sky,
Burning and melting anything in my path.
After I let go
My inside is full of sorrow again,
I moan till I slumber,
I sleep for thousands of years.
I'll be back with a moan,
I will let go again.

Martin Goodwin (10)
Abbey Lane Primary School

Tidal Wave

I can control the fate of any living thing,
Even the most mighty of creatures could not defeat the power of me,
I will destroy anything in sight and beyond.
If you treat me with contempt
I will erupt like a volcano.
I am the king of the legendary blue ocean,
Do not even try and think you have elite power over me,
Or your future will end up in chaos.
I am a god on this Earth
And if you think the beach is a peaceful place
Then you are very wrong!

Christopher Davis-Smith (11)
Abbey Lane Primary School

A Cheetah

Silent and quick like a speeding motor,
A whipping tail and flat, soft paws,
With mellow paws and polka dots as far as the eye can see,
His face wide and his tail narrow,
His athletic body leaps and pounces
While his glinting eyes keep locked on his prey,
His legs nimble but delicate,
He always keeps on going, doesn't even have a break,
He may look vicious to some people
But not to me,
He always looks friendly.

Sam Dickinson (11)
Abbey Lane Primary School

Potion Of Love

Heart of cat, song of bird,
The sweetest song you've ever heard.

Dust of fairy, tongue of dove,
All this love come from above.
Paws of kitten, bark of dog,
Feather of hen, snort of hog.

Wing of angel, wedding ring,
Every single beautiful thing.
Red of rainbow, the colour of heart,
All this love will never part.

Heart of teddy, ear of deer,
All in this gold dish over here.
Antennae of butterfly, hair of girl,
Wing of robin, a clam's pearl.

Heart of cat, song of bird,
The sweetest song you've ever heard.

Ellie Town (11)
Abbey Lane Primary School

Elements

Earth is our future,
It helps to grow our food,
Earth is our past,
It grew the trees for the birds,
Earth is our life element.

Air can be peaceful,
It can keep us cool with its breeze,
Air can be angry and restless,
Causing ultimate chaos around our world,
Air is an undecided element.

Fire is powerful,
It is a playful fiend,
Fire is something not to mess with,
It is almost invincible,
Fire is an outraged element.

Water can be calm,
It is a habitat to creatures small,
Water can be rough,
An enemy to all in its path,
Water is a two-minded element.

Ella Motuza (10)
Abbey Lane Primary School

Thunder And Lightning

I can stomp and stamp and boom
And I can sing a monstrous song!
When I get angry I can destroy things very easily.
Even though I am deadly, when I have passed the air is clear.
I can strike a tree down with no tools or string,
And when I bring rain it is easier for me to kill,
For I am lord of the skies!

Tom Hudson (11)
Abbey Lane Primary School

A Padded Paw Kenning

A padded paw,
A ripping claw.

A silent prowler,
A loud growler.

A golden mane,
A yellow flame.

A raw piece of meat,
A nice treat.

A swishing tail,
A deadly male.

A catalogue to make me
A lion.

Josephine Hobson (11)
Abbey Lane Primary School

The Moon

I can light the night with the sun behind my back,
I can sleep in the day when the visitors arrive,
I can change in winter and get darker and darker,
So when I look down I can see you and you can see me.
I can talk to the stars and read them little stories,
So when I'm up high I'm very happy.
I see rockets and shooting stars and even the sun in the day,
I look at my visitors that come from Earth,
They crawl and jump all over my belly.

Zoe Lipscomb (11)
Abby Lane Primary School

Ode To A Dinner Lady

Pickled onions, carrot cake,
Rotten bacon, broccoli bake,
Mouldy biscuits, manky cheese,
I say no to poisonous peas.
Crumbly pastry, celery, jam,
Please don't give me dinner lady ham.
Crippled eggs, scaly fish,
All the food a troll could wish,
Ancient pancakes, skin-covered custard,
Chocolate sauce that tastes like mustard,
Greasy chips that look like squid,
This scary meal is seven quid.
The evil things that lay in store,
Behind the cursed serving door,
Nick and Joe are very scared,
Behind the door we're not prepared.
The food is looking very shady,
We call it Ode To A Dinner Lady!

Joe Ironside & Nick Hudson (10)
Abbey Lane Primary School

A Volcano

I can fry life down to a skeleton,
I can turn trees to charcoal in just one touch,
I can stand still for ages and ages,
I can help warm up the sea,
My smoke can make night come early by covering the sky,
My lava trickles down my side,
I blow the lava out with one huge breath,
My breath sends out steam before my insides explode,
I create rivers in which you cannot swim.

Rachel Sellars (10)
Abbey Lane Primary School

There Was A Señorita From Spain

There was a señorita from Spain
Who liked to dance mostly in rain,
One day she got dizzy,
The pavement got slippy
And so she fell right down the drain!

Hope Marsden & Jordanne Maskrey (10)
Abbey Lane Primary School

Volcano

I explode unexpectedly,
I can sleep for hundreds of years.
I release molten rock
That destroys anything in my path.
I stand above anything for miles around.
I weave in and out of boulders and rocks.
I cannot be destroyed, only I can destroy.
I slither down the mountain and melt the sea.

Joseph Johnson (11)
Abbey Lane Primary School

Carbon Monoxide

I can seep through cracks where no one else fits,
And destroy my enemies in a giant blitz.

I can evacuate a building in all but an hour,
On this planet I have awesome power.

Fuel and petrol burn and I am created,
My destructive nature is often debated.

Joe Moulam (11)
Abbey Lane Primary School

Fire

I lick with my tongues of fire at all that is not wet,
I send heaps of smoke that float up into the heavens,
I eat away at wood burning it to a crisp
And I can demolish all your possessions with one wave of heat.
I can spit sparks all around and give off terrible warmth,
I will grow and spread forever if I am not put out.
I dance round the Earth as free as a bird can be
And roar and scream and burn I do,
Till my glowing flame is stopped.
Giving off warmth and light is part of my job
But eating up the world is my strength,
Silently I creep and I wreck anything in my path.

Ben Porter (10)
Abbey Lane Primary School

The Great Robbery

Peering from the bushes I see him coming,
As I walk past I can hear his sneaky humming.
When he approaches I tiptoe near,
To see what he's up to, it's not very clear.
As I reach the doorstep and look through the tree,
I see the birds, they're helplessly staring at me.
I realise what's wrong and march through the door,
But when I see him with a gun I fell to the floor.
He leaves me lying on the ground,
With stolen jewels I have found.
I take the jewels to the station
And they search all over the nation.
I am overjoyed when they identify him,
Until an evil comment comes from his son, Jim!
They are both behind bars when he insults the police
And when his relatives find out the most upset will be his niece.

Samantha Barton (10)
Anston Brook Primary School

The Chocolate Box

All wrapped up
Nice and neat,
To give to my mum
For her birthday treat . . .

But I open the box,
I just can't resist,
Can't choose what to have
So look at the list . . .

Galaxy, Snickers
With nuts galore,
I take a handful
And one or two more . . .

Dig my hand in the box,
Take a lucky dip,
Pull out a Bounty
And put it to my lip . . .

About to bite it,
When someone comes upstairs,
My mum opens the door
And catches me unawares . . .

Emily Haigh (10)
Anston Brook Primary School

School

School is . . .
Saying sorry when you've tripped up a teacher.
Catching up on the latest gossip,
Hating maths and English.
'Oh I didn't see you there.'
'Oh I like your hair.'
Love, when you get your first girlfriend or boyfriend!

Suzanne Machin (11) & Rebekah Jory (10)
Anston Brook Primary School

Once Upon A Rhyme

Once upon a rhyme,
There was a rose that never opened,
The smell of God's fresh hands,
Each new hot meal that I eat,
The sweet smell of honey.

Once upon a rhyme,
A sun that never stopped shining,
Stars that always twinkled in the night,
The planet Mars that changed different colours,
A mysterious land not yet discovered.

Once upon a rhyme,
School where every child learns,
A world full of peace,
Blue sea that flows calmly,
A place where love is real.

Bethany Fowkes (8)
Anston Brook Primary School

This Is My Family

This is my family, the ones that share and care,
The ones that love and hug,
Especially the ones that I adore.
They will be with me forever more,
Never would I leave them,
Never would they leave me.
The bond shall not be broken
For we are one.
We stand tall across the nation
With the love that keeps on growing,
Generation after generation.

Gemma Fox (11)
Anston Brook Primary School

My Family

My mum gives me lots of love.
My dad calls me a pain but he loves me.
My brother says I get on his nerves but he loves me.
My grandma tells me to stop it when I'm being annoying,
But she loves me.
They all love me and I love them.

Laura Tomlinson (11)
Anston Brook Primary School

Snow

Slowly, silently now the snow,
Making all the noses glow,
Sprinkling sugar over lakes,
Houses turned into birthday cakes.

Rebecca Amber Rose Dabill (8)
Anston Brook Primary School

The Wild West

My dad is a cowboy,
He rides through the plain.
He shoots the bandits,
He's really insane.

Although he likes to shoot,
He also has a weak side.
He always used to say,
'You can run but you can't hide.'

He's an American rodeo,
Riding through the woods.
He has gold and blue boots
With piercing studs.

Daniel Meigh (10)
Birdwell Primary School

Brother Bother Kenning

A hair puller,
A black colour,
A mischief machine,
Opposite of clean,
A bedroom wrecker,
A morning waker,
Object thrower,
Height is lower,
Boasting level
Sent from the Devil,
Troublemaker,
Sweet taker,
Dinner spitter,
Sister hitter!
Innocent eyes,
Always lies.

Tori Ellis Raynes (10)
Birdwell Primary School

The Sun Kenning

A bright light,
A blinding sight
In the sky,
Way up high,
Long beams,
Massive it seems,
The biggest star,
Quite far.

Melissa Parnham
Birdwell Primary School

Snow Kenning

An ice pile,
A slippy covering,
A graceful faller,
An easy builder,
A great shaper,
A shiver maker,
A finger freezer,
A white blanket.

Laura Fenton (11)
Birdwell Primary School

Tanka

Winter snow falling,
Hedgehogs curl up in their balls,
They're prickly and short,
Under the paper-white snow
Laid down on green grass asleep.

George Ainsley Addy (10)
Birdwell Primary School

Tanka

On my way to sea
I stopped and bought an ice cream,
Dropped it in the car
And my mum started to scream,
We stopped and got another.

Nicola Cox (11)
Birdwell Primary School

Manor!

We are going to the manor,
'Have a good time,' said Nanna.
I am going to bed late
And I am going with my mate.

I am going to get up early
And my hair will be curly.
I am going to do rock climbing
And I and my friend are going to do miming.

I am going to have a good time,
We are setting off at nine.
I can't wait!
I can't wait!

Emma Simpson (10)
Brampton Ellis CE Junior School

I Think I'm Perfect

My mum, my dad,
They're both so silly.
My dad says I'm bad,
My mum says I'm mad,
But I think I'm not,
I just think I'm perfect!

Abbie Pattison (10)
Brampton Ellis CE Junior School

Troublesome Tower

One day I went to explore,
There was a big and creaky door,
Plus no light,
It gave me a fright,
Then I fell through the floor.

Daniel Howell (10)
Brampton Ellis CE Junior School

Atlantic

A vast seascape of brilliant blue.
T he sound of the crashing waves against the coast line.
L and a mere speck on the horizon.
A t last another ship within range of the sails.
N ever tired are the birds, wheeling overhead.
T edious is the groaning of the hull.
I n the hold the barrels roll.
C old is the air near the home port.

Christopher Rigby (11)
Brampton Ellis CE Junior School

The Wrath Of The Evil Underpants

They suck you in so tight,
It really gives you a fright.
You don't know when they will next strike,
They're the underpants you won't like.
They're the underpants from Hell,
You can't stand the smell.
So if you see them coming down the street,
Remember they're the underpants you don't want to meet!

Leigh Marrow (10)
Brampton Ellis CE Junior School

The Fox

Fast and slim,
Tearing down prey's flesh,
In darkness or light,
There it hunts
For its meat,
And then . . .
It pounces
And kills!

Josh Evers (10)
Brampton Ellis CE Junior School

My Lotto Dream

I'd love to win the lottery,
I'd buy all kinds of things,
Like a mansion in Australia
And lots of diamond rings.

I would buy a great big speedboat
And go racing across the sea,
I'd maybe buy a little goat
And a puppy or three.

But it will probably never come true
Because it is just my Lotto dream.

Amy Graham (11)
Brampton Ellis CE Junior School

Don't Wee In The Bath, Terry

Don't wee in the bath, Terry,
It makes the water turn yellow,
It's also unhygenic,
For you're a young fellow.

Don't sing in the bath, Pink,
It makes the house shake,
You really don't think
But our house will break!

Josh Moore (11)
Brampton Ellis CE Junior School

Crime Time

Once upon a time
A man committed crime.
He stole from the bank
And bought a tank,
How dare he do such a crime?
(Now he's doing time.)

Dillon Harris (11)
Brampton Ellis CE Junior School

A Sister's Love

2.22am my baby brother was born,
He fell asleep after a wide yawn.
He was named Marshall Owen,
He is such a little darlin'.
Nursed about, eating and sleeping,
The first time I met him with joy my heart was leaping.
I wanted a sister but I don't mind,
I've got a baby brother to whom I'm kind.
He is now my baby brother,
Born to a proud family where we love each other.
He owns a lot of strong love,
Because he means peace better than a dove.

Charissa Leigh Garner (10)
Brampton Ellis CE Junior School

The Boy Called Tim

There was once a boy called Tim
Who scavenged around in a dustbin.
He once found some money
And bought some honey,
That was once the boy called Tim.

There was once a girl called May
Who was related to Tim in a way.
She ate Tim's honey
And paid him no money,
That was the fat girl called May.

Thomas Lelliott (11)
Brampton Ellis CE Junior School

School Is So Cool

School is so cool,
We all stick together, we do,
We all work hard, we do,
Oh school is so cool.

We all play together, we do,
Everybody is so cool,
We all stick together, we do,
Oh school is so cool.

Teachers are so good,
They work hard all day,
Looking after us for little pay,
Oh school is so cool.

Christina is my best friend,
She's there all the day,
Oh what a good friend she is,
Oh school is so *cool!*

Natalie Vardy (11)
Brampton Ellis CE Junior School

Zoom! Zoom!

S uper bikes *rock*,
U tter amazement grasped the crowd,
P erformance brakes the lock,
E ndurance is the key,
R acing is a pride.

B est rider
I s admired,
K ick start zooms,
E ngaged gears.

Ryan Jackson (11)
Brampton Ellis CE Junior School

Monsters

Are there monsters under the bed,
That's what I want to know?
But one night I was about to go to sleep,
When I saw something strange
And ugly at the end of my toes.
Then, when I looked I had quite a shock,
When I saw it was just my brother's old dirty sock.

Luke Johnson (11)
Brampton Ellis CE Junior School

Bad Luck

There was an old man from Shieling,
He had a peculiar feeling.
He laid on his back,
Heard a tick-tack
And on his head, fell the ceiling.

He was in social care
When he saw a grizzly bear,
It bit off his head
And now he is dead,
Now that's peculiar hair!

Jordan Wood (10)
Brampton Ellis CE Junior School

The Sun Is A . . . ?

The sun is a missile puncturing the Earth's surface.
The sun is a fire soothing on a winter's day.
The sun is a giant rose with a sweet aroma.
The sun is a sword punishing the people on Earth.

Luke Theaker (10)
Brampton Ellis CE Junior School

I Really Want A Dog!

I really want a dog,
I really, really do.
I'd play with it all day and night
And I'd clean up all its poo!

I'd call it Max,
Max is his name.
He might chew up my slipper,
Then he'd hang his head with shame.

He'd love to come on holiday,
In our car he would.
He'd sit still and be very quiet,
Just like he should.

He'd be the best dog ever,
Better than any other.
He'd follow me everywhere,
Just like a little brother!

Laura Clarkson (10)
Brampton Ellis CE Junior School

Tim And Tom

There was an old dog called Tim,
Who was the opposite of slim,
He slept all the day
And at night he wanted to play,
That silly old dog called Tim.

There was a young cat called Tom,
Who loved to chase after a pom-pom,
He ate lots of food
And when he was in the mood
He slept next to Tim, did Tom.

Rebecca Brown (11)
Brampton Ellis CE Junior School

Gamers' World

The TV flashes in the darkness,
The thumb's upon the joypad,
The cheat book lying on the floor,
I dare not pick it up.
'I'm on the last level, I'm on the last level,
I cheated all the way!'

Josh Caddick (10)
Brampton Ellis CE Junior School

Dusty

Dusty stands in his grey old field,
His legs and limbs ache from his young days.
His head hangs over the old disintegrating fence,
In his mind he sees carriages with loaves of bread.
Poor old Dusty, poor old Dusty.

Brooke Gale (10)
Brampton Ellis CE Junior School

The Three Kings From Leicester Square!

We three kings from Leicester Square,
Selling women's underwear,
It's fantastic,
No elastic,
A wonderful sight they are!

Oliver Banks (11)
Brampton Ellis CE Junior School

The Yew Fantasy (But It's Really Reality)

Typical there they go again,
Starting to complain.
Pulling funny faces,
Pretending to run races.
Soon they might fall,
Look at them all!

Michael and Neil laughing at one of their jokes,
Emily and Rhian pretending to be old folks.

Thomas Perrie being stupid, Simon showing off,
Hannah can't stop jumping with every hacking cough.

Isobel's drawing on the walls, Jake's picking his nose,
Jodi's took her socks off to reveal her smelly toes.

Barbara and Jade are silently whispering,
Nichola and Jasmine's just made Toni sing.

Thomas Oxby and Thomas Barns fighting both together,
Leaving Mrs Webb at the end of her tether.

Olivia and Sarah bickering over nothing,
Oh no not again! Kyle's eating crisps that are ringed.

Ryan Hogg's picking on Ashley, who's cowering in fear,
Rebecca Wright and Becky Hockey looking really queer.

Victoria and James giggling,what for I don't know,
Nathan and Jonathon put their bellies on show.

Ryan Mitchell and Lindsey running round the room,
If they don't stop Mrs Webb will send them to their doom.

Alex and Connor as stupid as can be,
And then of course there's little young me.

Sat in a corner doing nothing at all,
I think it'll be disaster if Mrs Dobson comes to call.

If that happens they'll get a beating from their heads to their knees,
Remember it really is reality and not fantasy.

Laura Jean Keetley (11)
Dinnington Primary School

School Prom

Laura and Thomas at the back kissing,
Simon and Emily they've gone missing.
Tom P he's the DJ,
Jonathan's come in his PJs.
Connor and Olivia doing a dance,
Oh I remembered Emily's in France.
Jodi and Bushy having a giggle,
Isobel and Neil doing the wiggle,
Barbara and Alex stood by the punch bowl,
Jade and Jake are covered in moles.

Hannah Gregory (11)
Dinnington Primary School

School Teachers Acrostic

S cary teachers
C an always use the word angry
H ollow minds
O bservant eyes
O pine thinkers
L osing control.

T eachers think they rule
E volving from chimpanzees
A nd some, well probably an ant
C lever but thick
H aving a good time
E ven on a Friday
R acing intelligence
S o scary!

Thomas Perrie (10)
Dinnington Primary School

The Sounds Of The Classroom

The sounds of the classroom
Go all through the school,
The cry of the children
That say it's not cool.
The cheer today
For the sports day winner,
Tired and hungry,
Come in for their dinner.
The rumble of bellies
As dinner goes in,
The crunch of the people
Who eat by the bin.
The yelp of the children
That play on the grounds,
The zoom of the children
That run out of bounds.
The slam of the door
At the home time bell's ring,
The children all think
What the next day might bring.

Neil Fletcher (10)
Dinnington Primary School

Dragon

D emon! Devil!
R iotous beast!
A geless eyes of granite.
G orgon! Killer! Fire from above.
O ppressive fiend, tyrant king.
N ight, on wings of leather.

Jacob Robinson (10)
Dinnington Primary School

At The Bonfire

Can you see it?
No!
Can you hear it?
Yes!
The crackle of sparkles,
The rumble of a fire,
The whoosh of the rocket
That burst a tyre,
The scream of the children
That seem very scared,
The people are dressed
Up in many layers,
The oooh of the crowd
At the bang of the rocket,
There is a big whizz
As I look in my pocket,
As we say goodnight
The sound grows quiet,
As I reach home
I can still hear the riot,
The sounds of the fifth fade
As I get into my bed,
Until next year the sound
I'll hear in my head.

Simon Wagstaff (11)
Dinnington Primary School

Anger

Anger is red as blood,
It smells like smoke from a fire.
Anger tastes like moulding food,
It sounds like a rattling steam train,
It feels like death and fear.
Anger lives in people.

Kyle Downs (11)
Dinnington Primary School

Teacher's Ill

Oh no! Teacher's ill,
We've now got a teacher named Mr Bill.
He used to be a policeman you know,
He taught us how the river used to flow
Until his white skin turned a pale brown,
Mr Bill is now the class clown.
Honestly he's a nightmare,
Oh how the children look and stare
At his wife, she looks so weird,
If you look closer she's got a beard.
They look at his T-shirt,
It looks so much like a mini skirt.
Finally it's the end of today,
I hope we haven't got him for another day.

Rebecca Page (10)
Dinnington Primary School

My Magical Ways

M ysterious ways
A bracadabra
G oing, going, going, gone
I mpossible tricks
C ourageous magician
A bsolutely magnificent
L ively as can be.

W eekly shouts
A ctivities free
Y uletide shows
S uitable for all.

Rhian Richardson (10)
Dinnington Primary School

Football

F our great saves by the keeper
O oo go the crowd,
O w goes the goalkeeper,
T ruly magnificent save,
B lasting shot hits the bar,
A ll the shots are going wide,
L osers and winners,
L ive on TV.

Alex Keeton (10)
Dinnington Primary School

Dolphin

D ancing creature
O cean swimmer
L ively flyer
P erfect dancer
H igh jumper
I ntelligent hunter
N ice kisser.

Emily Skill (11)
Dinnington Primary School

Dolphins

D iving in the waving sea
O val bodies swimming silently through the water
L ong distance swimmers
P eople say they are loveable creatures
H elpful and graceful
I mpressive swimmers
N arrowly missing
S harp rocks, diving, swirling, swimming.

Barbara Maia (11)
Dinnington Primary School

Class Photo

He's ugly,
She's thick,
He's going to be sick.

Her hair's a mess,
My teacher's weird,
She's growing a beard.

He's too fat,
She's too thin,
Look at her ugly twin.

She's annoying,
He's a pain,
That's my friend Jane.

I hate him,
Look at her boot,
The word to describe me is cute!

Chloe Hamilton (10)
Dinnington Primary School

On The Sea Near France

Being on the sea near France
You should go there if you get the chance,
It's a lovely place to be,
Just floating there on the sea,
Dolphins jumping,
Waves bumping,
Such a lovely trip on the sea near France,
So fast, like a pack of cheetahs,
Running over 10,000 litres,
Being near the place they call France.

Ashley Johnson (10)
Dinnington Primary School

Goldilocks And The Three Bears

Once there were three big bears,
With great big claws and a lot of hairs.
Mummy Bear, Daddy Bear, Baby Bear too,
They acted fierce like all bears do.
Mummy Bear made some porridge one day,
So they left it to cool and went away.
In came Goldilocks to the three bears' house,
She came in quietly like a very small mouse.
She saw the porridge on the table top,
One was too cold and one was too hot.
Baby Bear's porridge was to her just right,
So she went upstairs to the room for the night.
In that room there was a small bed,
Just the right size to rest her head.
The bears got home and they were completely mad,
Baby Bear was very sad.
They went upstairs, chased Goldilocks away,
No more mischief from Goldilocks today.

Ashley Wilde (11)
Dinnington Primary School

War

War is black,
It smells like smoke after a blazing fire.
War sounds like swords gashing in hearts,
It feels like my skin's burning.
War tastes like blood.
War lives in the heart of some dragons.

Jake Whitworth (10)
Dinnington Primary School

There's A Snow Cloud Coming

Cloud is big,
Crunchy snowflakes,
Big ice melting,
There's a snow cloud coming.

Slimy ice
Melting fast,
Sloppy snow,
There's a snow cloud coming.

Icy grass,
Hard icicles,
Snowmen falling,
There's a snow cloud coming.

Frosty ice,
Snow rumbling,
Snowballs crunchy,
There's a snow cloud coming.

Nathan Gregory (9)
Dinnington Primary School

Dog Kenning

Treat taker,
Loud barker,
Nosy parker,
High jumper,
Hole digger,
Happy smiler.

People lover,
Book chewer,
Tail wagger,
Cat chaser,
Good tormentor,
Fast runner.

Nichola Tongue (10)
Dinnington Primary School

Biking

Watch the bikers bike along, biking fast with no wrong,
Fighting the sandstorm brave and strong,
Also killing the biting bears,
Getting faster and faster biking along.

I go riding on my bike,
The wheels go round and round,
Going up and down the hills,
Travelling over bumpy ground.

Holding on the handlebars,
Travelling over hills afar,
Enjoying lovely summer breeze,
Riding along through the trees.

Nick Hobson (10)
Everton Primary School

A Wild Winter

The wind was rushing,
The flowers had gone,
The river was gushing,
Some people were skating but not everyone.

Most of them lying in their beds
With drowsy and tired, sniffly heads,
Their boxes of tissues by their sides,
The winter ghoul's eyes bright open wide.

The winter ghoul groans bang on midnight
While everyone's snoring,
It freezes the living and brings in the dead
While everyone's trying to get out of bed!

Harriet Arden (11)
Everton Primary School

Blazing Fire

Fire blazes and lights up
The midnight sky, brightening
Up all the dark,
Sparks flying with warmth
And heat with a warm strength.

Blazing fire fighting fearlessly
With strength and might.
Melting snow of all amounts,
Never going, never coming.
Fire burning, blazing high,
Harshly burning towards the sky.

Fire burning, bright burning,
Warmth burning with no
Fear, never without strength.
Fire blazing and burning down trees.
Destroying anything in
Its random path of destruction.

Fire starts small then grows
And grows,
Bigger until it's blazing
High with choking smoke that reaches
Up and up, until burning
Everything high or low.
Until flickering with a
Small flame with no smoke,
Just burnt wood.

Adam Knight (10)
Everton Primary School

Snake

A scaly snake
Slithers through the trees,
As long as a rake
And guess what it sees?
A mouse running away
On a bright, sunny day.

A scaly snake
Slithers through the forest,
As long as a lake
And guess what it spots?
A rabbit running away
On a cold, rainy day.

A scaly snake
Slithers by the creek,
As pretty as a cake
And guess what it seeks?
A bird flying away
On a scary, windy day.

A scaly snake
Slithers through the rain
Without a squeak
And guess what it gets?
No tea for a week!

Roisin Tasker (9)
Everton Primary School

Animals

A nts waiting by the pool,
N ewts in the pond getting cool.
I guanas in the hot, hot jungle, huddled up in a bundle.
M onkeys swinging from tree to tree,
A pes peering up to see.
L ions out in the rain,
S nakes slithering on the plains.

Meghan O'Connor (10)
Everton Primary School

Otter

Dip otter dip,
Swim otter swim,
Dive otter dive,
Shining like a star,
Swimming very far,
Oh I wish I was an otter.
Bob otter bob,
Eat otter eat,
They get a rock and a clam
And bang, bang, bang,
Chew otter chew,
Munch otter munch,
Crunch, crunch, crunch.

Christopher Deakin (8)
Everton Primary School

Sea Beast, Sea Beast

Making the sea shake,
Crashing against the side,
Tearing the rocks apart.

Waiting for rain splashing
And crashing down from the dark
And gloomy sky.

Making the sea fearsome,
So don't get wet in the shivery sea.

Cold and wet and slippery
Broken rocks.

Jack Rowe (10)
Everton Primary School

Wind-Beast

In the moonlight shadow
He runs and he walks,
In the light and thrashing rain
He stands and he talks.

He sees no light
And also no day,
And still he comes,
Can't stay away.

North and south,
West and east
And there he goes,
My blowing wind-beast.

Evangelene Oxley (11)
Everton Primary School

The Ocean

The ocean waves rushing like mad,
So strong they knock you over.
The water singing like in a choir.
The waves can get so mad,
They reach ten feet high.
The ocean, the ocean,
Swirling, twirling, rushing all around,
Come any closer and you'll die.

You'll be underwater for the rest of your life.
The whirlpool ranting, raving, swirling never stops,
Always going in circles just like life,
It keeps on going round, it's a beautiful sight.
The golden sand, the dark blue ocean,
Just seeing the waves rush on the sand.
The tide going in and out,
You hear the seagulls
And you just sit there watching it
Make that *sshhh* sound.

Daniel Stafford (9)
Everton Primary School

Ocean

Ocean is vicious, breaks out of its cage,
Ocean is angry and full of rage,
Sea is coming down in a massive wave,
Putting to a watery grave.

It's coming as fast as a runner in a race,
Leaving not a single trace.
It will destroy everything in its path,
Because it is an evil ocean, full of wrath.

The beast of the sea rips at the rocks,
Charging like an angry ox,
Scaring people out of their socks,
Whilst destroying the wooden docks.

Will Shaw (11)
Everton Primary School

Winter

Winter has come,
Summer has gone
To freeze us again.
'Put on your coats,
Hat, scarf and gloves,'
Our mums shout.
We throw snowballs
At each other,
We build snowmen.
Mother Nature says,
'That's enough, now
It's time for spring.'
The year starts all over again.

Daniella Bradshaw (8)
Goldthorpe Primary School

Cheetahs

Cheetahs are a speedy animal,
They will bite you,
Their teeth are white,
They will give you a fright,
Their teeth are bright,
They have no fear,
Coming down on the hillside they purr,
When it rains or shines, even worse snow,
They love it all the time - they will live.

Kyle Calder (8)
Goldthorpe Primary School

Under Sea

The sunset rose, the dolphin jumps over the sun,
Wet fins jump back into the water,
Can you see the mermaid on the rocks waving with her crinkly hands?
The shark raging around like a nutter,
The ray fish is very floppy,
The whale opens its huge mouth and eats the tiny krill.

Chelsea Beighton (9)
Goldthorpe Primary School

My Little Monkey

My little monkey
Eats bananas and bugs.
My little monkey,
His name is Hugbug.
My little monkey
Runs like a nutter.
My little monkey
Loves me and you.

Christopher Gillatt (9)
Goldthorpe Primary School

A Man Flew Away

One old day a man flew away,
He flew to Italy and Spain,
But when he got to France he started to dance in the windy rain.
He flew to the moon and he flew to Mars,
When he got home there were flying cars.
There were flying people just like him that had flown to Italy
and flown to Spain.
I'm not going through it again cos they did exactly the same!

Dale Cook (9)
Goldthorpe Primary School

Sammy The Snowman

Sammy the snowman is so cold,
He has a cold, stony mouth
And a black big hat that's fluffy,
He's fat with eyes as rocky as rocks
And a nose as a fizzy bottle cap.

Reese Spiller (8)
Goldthorpe Primary School

Valentine

V iolins play a beautiful tune,
A ll the time I look into your eyes. I see the stars
that sparkle all night long.
L ove is the best gift that anyone could have.
E legant roses stand next to me.
N ice and gorgeous, violets all around on the patio grounds.
T he times that we have are silent and loveable.
I see you standing at my door when we fall out.
N ew love is all around.
E asy nights with candlelight we have on this lovely night.

Jenna Neale (10)
Goldthorpe Primary School

Valentine's

V iolins play a silent riddle
A ll year round you need a fiddle
L ove is loving and sweet
E verlasting all year round
N ever ever make a sound
T ime is ending
I t is Valentine's Day
N ever ending your heart's bleeding
E veryone loves you
S o you're happy all year round.

Amy Kilner (9)
Goldthorpe Primary School

Valentine's Love

Valentine's Day is all about love,
All the love that's from above.
Valentine's Day is for loved ones only,
It can be for people that are single and lonely.

Valentine's Day is for special people too,
Think of all the love that's sent to you.
Valentine's Day is just for fun,
Think of all the love that you have won.

Brittany Beighton (9)
Goldthorpe Primary School

Love

Love is nice, love is sweet,
All I want is a kiss on the cheek.
On my cheek is a star.
Valentine is beautiful
Just like you.

Neil Todd (11)
Goldthorpe Primary School

Murder On Valentine's Day

One gloomy night on Valentine's Day
A girl comes out to play.
She comes out with glory,
Her name is Miss Dory.
A murderer comes out
To murder the girl
On the street.
She was scared to death,
She dashed into the house
And then she was safe.
She loved her mum
With all of her heart
So never go out at night.

Daniel Sargison (9)
Goldthorpe Primary School

Death Is Danger

D eath I hate,
E veryone's fate.
A romas great in the world,
T wo-faced bullies and stupid jerks,
H e's always gonna get killed.

I gloos cold and icy,
S enses warm and feisty.

D eath is horrible
A nd it is nasty.
N ever go into the night.
G inger ale is poison.
E lectric-blue I've got the flu,
R eaching into the light.

Dominic Kilner (10)
Goldthorpe Primary School

Sea Creatures

Sharks swift and drift, their teeth are scary,
Sharks are fierce, furious and not hairy.

Squids squelch on the seabed,
Swimming around with their slimy head.

Eels swivel and eels swerve,
Eels dive and eels curve.

Reece Weddell (11)
Goldthorpe Primary School

Valentine

V alentine is sweet
A ll year round
L ove is heart-breaking
E verlasting, beautiful love
N ever stops
T he red rosy flowers are given
I think Valentine is great
N obody has enough love
E verybody likes Valentine.

James Stevenson (10)
Goldthorpe Primary School

The Octopus

In the dark blue sea
There's an octopus called Lee.
He's very wavy and squashy,
His colour is navy.
He sounds like a baby,
He lives under the sea.
When he gets scared
He makes ink for me!

Liam Hollinshead (11)
Goldthorpe Primary School

Death Is Horrible

D eath is horrible,
E lephant-grey,
A nguish is painful,
T igers fierce,
H orrible days are the worst of death.

T ime to time are great,
I gloo cold, freezing gate,
M ining muck, digging through,
E lements lovely, so are you.

James Brice (10)
Goldthorpe Primary School

Valentine's Day

Beautiful flowers for Valentine's Day
Crush my heart because they are away.
Valentine's Day is a special day.
Roses at Valentine's Day stay next to me.
It's a happy day for me.

She got a loveable, cuddly bear,
Beautiful bear for Valentine's Day.
Valentine in the dark night,
My heart is broken, I can start again.

Abbie Morris (9)
Goldthorpe Primary School

Elephants

Elephants are funny and silly,
Their tusks are sharp and pointy.
Elephants are grey,
Elephants are normally at the zoo,
They meet together at night.
My elephant's called Snooker.

Joshua Cook (8)
Goldthorpe Primary School

There's Evil

There's evil somewhere,
I just know,
There's a house somewhere,
That's going to blow.

There's evil here,
There's evil there,
There's evil in the clouds
And there's evil in the air.

There's evil in the school
And evil at home,
And there's evil
In my dog's bone.

There's evil in computers
And evil in the bin,
There's evil in my bedroom
And there's evil in your skin.

Daniel Cadman (8)
Goldthorpe Primary School

Valentine

V alentine is loving, sweet and wonderful
A ll the year round
L ove is beautiful and heart-breaking
E verlasting love, liking
N ever-ending broken hearts
T he red rosy flowers are given
I think Valentine is appealing
N obody does enough kisses
E verybody loves Valentine.

James Jones (10)
Goldthorpe Primary School

Love

Love is sweet
On Valentine's Day.
People care for others
On lover's day.
People are never nasty
On lover's day.
I think this is a very special day.
I once had a girlfriend
But that was when I was three.
Her name was Kimberley
But I don't remember her,
I left when I was four!

Christopher Cadman (10)
Goldthorpe Primary School

The Snowy Owl

The snowy owl is like a star
Shimmering in space.

It sounds like the wind in the night,
It is as big as a boulder.

Its wings are like two silver crystals
All sparkling in the sky.

Its eyes are like small yellow gems
Sparkling in the sky.

It has stripes like a zebra,
Its beak is like two pieces of coal.

Stephen Barrett (10)
Goldthorpe Primary School

The Panda

The pandas are eating bamboo,
The pandas are having fun too.
As the pandas start to laze
The little ones have a craze.

It's the end of the day,
The pandas have nothing to say.
The pandas lay down to sleep,
Then a jeep starts to beep.

Then the pandas started to scurry
But the hunters shot the mother in a hurry.
The little one is left alone,
Scared and upset the little one started to moan.

Jessica Bywater (10)
Goldthorpe Primary School

The Sun

The sun sang silently as it
Reflected on the lake.

The sun dived deeply into
The muddy puddle.

The sun skidded smoothly
On the icy pond.

The sun swam softly in the
Bright green grass.

The sun danced delicately on
The shimmering shop window.

The sun slept safely on the
Comfy cloud.

Adam Stevenson (11)
Goldthorpe Primary School

The Cheetah In A Cage

The speeding cheetah in a cage
Prowls in the sun,
And in his mind he thinks
Of a life where he can run.

His baby face gets shouted at
So he growls in great fear.
He wants to be out hunting gazelles
Not in a dump like here.

He then imagines paradise
Racing at the speed of light.
He thinks of prey being feasted upon
And sleeping silently at night.

He then thinks of a way
To get out of this hell.
And soon he's out on the plains
Chasing those grey gazelles.

Thomas Jane (11)
Goldthorpe Primary School

What Is A Snowflake?

The snowflake is an empty milk bottle
With little tiny drops coming out.

It is a tiny cloud waiting to be eaten
From a candy stall.

It falls like white crumbs from an
Ice-cold cloud in the sky above me.

The snowflakes up in the sky
Falling steadily down onto me.

Hannah Clifton (10)
Goldthorpe Primary School

The Sea Creatures

Sharks swimming fast through the ocean,
Spilling their horrible potion.
A squid swirling and twisting slowly
And he is very lonely.
A sea snake slithering and slimy
Eating his prey lively.
The eels wait and look very fast
As the fishermen start to cast.
As a fish swims in the ocean it starts very funny
And people pay lots of money.

Lewis Dabell (11)
Goldthorpe Primary School

What Is The Sun?

The sun is a golden clock face
Waiting for the time to be changed.

It is a giant tennis ball
Ready to be hit to the opponent.

The sun is a yellow lemon
Wanting to be peeled.

It is a huge orange,
Wanting to be eaten.

Gabrielle Bousfield (11)
Goldthorpe Primary School

Squid

A
squishy,
squashy squid,
speeding through
the sea. Once I went
near one, it nearly hit
me. I dived out of
the way, really
really quick. Then
it came back again
so I hit it with a stick.

Kara Hall (10)
Goldthorpe Primary School

Sea Creatures

As the peaceful dolphin so
Sparkly and pretty twirls
Near the bottom of the ocean
You can see a chest of pretty pearls.

With the fast and fierce sharks that bite
And the squids that fight.

The little sea horse bouncing
And jumping in the middle of the ocean,
Near the sharks that drop evil potions.

Faye Miller (11)
Goldthorpe Primary School

My Mad Family!

My family is so mad you would not believe!
So I'll tell you shall I?
My sister is so bossy you have to do her chores!
Oh and there's my brother, he stays in his bedroom
Listening to his music *full blast!*
My mum is weird, she always has the Hoover out - weird!
My dad he falls asleep on the sofa
And sits on the toilet 10 hours a day!
And there's me so tired I don't speak, I'm not weird of course!

Hollie Chapman (8)
Goldthorpe Primary School

My Little Monkey

My little monkey scampers from vine to vine,
Tree trunk to tree trunk
And he's keen to follow you,
If you're passing by beware of the zoo,
You may end up with him on you.
He may touch your hair
For all those horrible things,
He'll give you a fright but he won't hurt you
Because he's my little monkey.

Samantha Sanderson (10)
Goldthorpe Primary School

Under The Sea

Under the sea, under the sea,
What a beautiful place to be,
See the octopus wiggle and whirl
Past the oysters up pops the pearl.
See the dolphin take a hurl,
Here come the fish, see the starfish slurp
And slop
And never stop,
Under the sea,
What a beautiful place to be.

Emma Townend (9)
Goldthorpe Primary School

Sea Creatures

The fantastic dolphin friendly and funny,
Swimming quicker than a bunny.

The nasty shark speedy and scary,
Massive and wild so don't be a fairy.

The big whale arrogant and aggressive,
Enormous, mad, sending out a message.

The kind mermaid pretty and calm,
Nice and peaceful with kindness in her palm.

Corey Butler (11)
Goldthorpe Primary School

The Sun

The sun fell off the cloud
But managed to land on her feet.

When she had eaten her food
She went back out to play.
But she became angry
For the rain was visiting
And she didn't want to stay.

The rain threw her about
And shoved her in the river
With her friend, the trout.

The sun didn't like this at all
So she came up with a plan
To give the rain a blistering suntan.

Jade Ratcliffe (10)
Goldthorpe Primary School

What Is Lightning?

The lightning is a cheetah
Running down to Earth.

It is a candle
Glowing up in the sky.

The lightning is a football
Being kicked by a player.

Lightning is a spectacular flame
In a black bag.

Matthew Quinn (10)
Goldthorpe Primary School

The Stables

It's morning,
I get up yawning.
I go to the stables.
Titch, Pepper, Cam, Crystal,
They're running up the field.
You can hear them cantering.
You can hear them galloping,
Crash, bang.
They run into me.
Crystal bucking,
Cam jumping,
Pepper standing there with Titch.
I open their door,
They walk in.
Crystal stops,
Cam stops,
They wait.
I open their door,
They walk in.
I walk into Pepper and Titch.
I give them their food,
Crystal looks,
Cam looks,
I give them their food.
'Rebecca,'
My friend shouts.
It's Georgia.
We brush the ponies,
We put the saddles on,
Then we go for a ride.

Rebecca Toone (10)
Grenoside Community Primary School

Haunted House

I opened the creaking door,
I stepped in, I couldn't stop my teeth from chattering,
I kept thinking what this was for,
This morning I thought I was indeed dying.

It sounded like a *thud*,
I thought I could see people floating,
I remembered my friends outside playing,
It smelt like dried, mucky mud,
This place was frightening me,
I kept seeing scary sights.

Abigail Ruston (10)
Grenoside Community Primary School

Summertime

The sun is warm,
The blue sky is clear,
Everyone is happy
Now summer is here.

Children are playing
Out in the park,
It is hours yet
Before it gets dark.

Lollies and ice cream
We have by the pool,
When it gets hot,
We'll jump in to keep cool.

Harry Davison (10)
Grenoside Community Primary School

The Haunting

There is a house which I live near,
One that everybody around does fear.

But one day I was dared
To go into the house that scared
Everyone in our village stiff -
And makes their hair stand up in a quiff.

'They're alright,' I said to myself in fear,
'They can stay their distance and not come near,'
But I had to go in
To the house full of sin.

As soon as I walked in the room,
I thought I was in for my doom.
Every floorboard I stood on creaked,
Then I looked up and I shrieked.
There was writing on the wall, ever so clear,
Which seemed to slowly draw you near,
Reading:
'I am the haunting!'

Della Newton (10)
Grenoside Community Primary School

Town

Cars not getting very far
As the teeming traffic comes to a halt.
Desperate drivers beep their horns in frustration.
The smell of fast food
Tells you you've arrived in town.
Tall towers, some with shiny steel,
Scaffolding looms over frantic faces,
Busy, bustling people jostle
To get into shops.
Mothers pushing their baby in a pram,
Struggling to get aboard a train.

Matthew Phipps (10)
Grenoside Community Primary School

A Day At The Farm

'Cock-a-doodle-do,' cried the large brown cock,
The farmer pulled on his long thick sock.
On the kitchen table were a large pile of eggs,
The farmer's dog sits near and begs.

The tractor stands in the big brown shed,
While animals appear from their cosy beds.
He can see the horses eating the hay,
And thinks to himself *what a wonderful day*.

The birds are flying really high,
You'd almost think they were touching the sky.
The farmer works all day long,
Merrily humming cheerful songs.

The daytime fades and the jobs are done,
The farmer returns to his wife and young son.
After supper he retires to bed,
Says his prayers and lays down his head.

Jessica Brennan (10)
Grenoside Community Primary School

My Day At Meadowhall

I went to Meadowhall today.
The hustle and bustle was there to stay.
I went into my fave shop.
Whilst my mom looked for a mop.

I tried on a skirt it was too tight.
My mom stormed in and had a fight.
'Can't find a mop.
Get out of this shop.
We're going home!'

Brady Edwards (10)
Grenoside Community Primary School

Wintertime

Winds whistle and whisper
Whirling through wintry white woods.

Icy path outside sparkles
Gleaming snow covers roads and lanes,
Jack Frost paints swirling patterns
On frosty windowpanes.

Inside, fire crackles
And looking out there,
See the snow falling, falling
Onto tree branches bare.

Robin redbreast hops outside
In the crisp and even snow,
We sit round the warm, warm fire
Warming up our cold, cold toes.

Children laughing and shouting
Sledging down the snowy roads,
Come inside and drink hot cocoa
With some tasty marshmallows.

Icicles with trembling droplets
Scattered here and there,
Ivy and holly with glossy red berries
Decorate everywhere.

Wintertime brings Christmas
Hang a stocking on my bed,
I know I will awake to find it
Full of gifts wrapped in gold and red.

Rachel Hurst (9)
Grenoside Community Primary School

The Playground

Ring, ring
The school bell rings for the playground,
Children come rushing out,
Shouting things about
Footy and a bacon buttie,
Playtime has begun.

Ring, ring
The school bell rings for playtime,
Children chatter,
Teachers natter,
School equipment goes with a clatter
Playtime has begun.

Laura L A Harrison (10)
Grenoside Community Primary School

Snow

There's nothing wrong with snow,
It's there with a winter's blow.
Sit by the fire,
Spring's nearly here.

Build a snowman fast,
And longer it will last.
Pack yourself up warm,
I'm sure there won't be a snowstorm.

The streets have turned all white,
It's time to fly your kite.
Snowball fights are the best,
No need to take a rest.

Winter comes and goes,
Not long until it snows.

Chelsey Deighton (10)
Grenoside Community Primary School

The Countryside

The countryside is a beautiful place,
It calms and relaxes you.
The dry green grass,
The delightful smell of red roses.

You need to walk up there to see the villages and cities.
The nice windy breeze,
The gorgeous blue sky,
Wind whistles like a bird.

You can't miss out,
Or you'll miss the dry green grass,
The delightful smell of red roses
And the gorgeous blue sky!

Natalie Bamforth (10)
Grenoside Community Primary School

Football

I kick my football up the street
Thinking who I could be . . .
Maybe an Owen?
Or even a
Rooney?
I decide to be a Beckham
I think of a free kick and bend it round
The wall
Smash!
The ball has gone through a window
And never seen again.

Greg Marshall (10)
Grenoside Community Primary School

The House Of Horror

You see the house of horror
And your hair stands on end
The ghoulish ghosts are cackling
When you turn the bend

You walk through the gruesome gardens
Through the swishing trees
And though the wind stopped whistling
You feel a quiver in your knees

When you enter the house of horror
And descend the squeaking stair
You'll find an endless corridor
With no door or window there

You pelt back down the staircase,
Sprint across the room
Yank the squeaking door open
And stand where the shadows loom

Yet as you walk across the gardens
You wonder even more
What is at the bottom
Of that endless corridor!

Lydia Beaumont (10)
Grenoside Community Primary School

Football Crazy

Racing down the wing
I score that goal
Everybody cheers like mad
They jump up and down shouting
Loud and clear, 'Put the ball in here!'

Kaylee Beth Hardy (10)
Grenoside Community Primary School

Spain

The waves smacking
on the crystal clear
water and the tropical
fish spring through the sea
the smell of paella
of the dusty beaches

the rusty railing
the painted sky
the watercolour sun
a dented pie
the smell of fish and chips.

Harry Rosewarne (10)
Grenoside Community Primary School

Grenoside Wood

My favourite wood is Greno' Wood
rustly leaves walk, red and orange leaves.

My favourite wood is Greno' Wood
horses passing by, the smell of horses is beautiful.

My favourite wood is Greno' Wood
The conkers falling off the trees collecting as you go.

My favourite wood is Greno' Wood
people with their dogs with them.

My favourite wood is Greno' Wood
I wonder if I'll find a better wood?
I wonder.

Ryan Marritt (10)
Grenoside Community Primary School

Trip To The Park

I go to the park
But not when it's dark,

I like to sing
When I'm on the creaking swing

But when I'm on the slippery slide
I see the planes glide

Sometimes when I go to the park
I hear dogs growl and bark

An hour or two has passed
I had better get home fast

My trip to the park did not last
Now it's a memory in the past

The park tomorrow will be the same
I'm very glad I came.

Larni Baverstock (10)
Grenoside Community Primary School

The Park

I sit on the slippy slide
I sit on the swishing swing
I sit on the springy grass
And I sit with you

I see fit footballers
I see bossy boys
I see giggling girls
And I see you.

Rebecca Holmes (10)
Grenoside Community Primary School

In The Park

As the wind blows,
The river flows,
The leaves rustle on the trees
And birds flutter in the breeze.

Children screaming,
1, 2, 3
Licking lollies joyfully.

The children are playing in the park
And do not realise it is getting dark,
As they slide down the slippery slide,
The birds fly around and glide.

It is getting late,
Everyone has gone through the gate
I'm left alone,
I want to go home.

Alex Livett (10)
Grenoside Community Primary School

The Old Haunted House

The haunted house . . .
The haunted house . . .
Creaking and banging
In the old haunted house
No one around
No one there
But still
Bang!
Smash!
In the old haunted house . . .

Joe Scholey (11)
Grenoside Community Primary School

My Trip To Disneyland

People, people everywhere,
Tourists, children young and old.
See the characters one and all,
Friendly families meet all Americans.

You can hear the loveable laughing,
The screeching screaming of people riding.
Painful crying from tired toddlers,
Little arguments of when to go home.

Lots of different places to be visited,
Disney Quest, Florida mall, water parks and Epcot.
Disneyland, Diners, MGM Studios, and in all the different places
You can hear the whooshing, swishing of the rides.

Smells of something sugary,
Chocolate, sweets and lollipops,
Fresh air wafting, the smell of
Bacon, burgers and greasy chips.

I squibble and squabble,
And shout, 'No, I don't want to go!;
My mum says, 'The flight's due tonight.'
I squiggle and squirm and still say
'No, I don't want to go!'

Lauren Bilby (10)
Grenoside Community Primary School

At The Park

I go to the park all day
And all I do is play
All I do is play ball
Until my mum gives me a call
On my way home I walk on the wall
And just hope I don't fall

I go to the park all day
And all I do is play
I play on the swings
Until my phone rings then I'm on my way

I have been in the park all day
And all I have done is play
It is now time I went home and got fed
Then get myself tucked up in bed

I have had a good time
In the park today.

Benjamin Gregory (10)
Grenoside Community Primary School

The Planet Of Cats

Manx is a cat with no tail.
Poison is a cat that looks like a fur ball.
Tabby is a cat with short fur.
Tortoise cat has fur like a shell.
Tigers with black and orange stripes
It reminds me of this beautiful light.
Lions are fierce with their shaggy mane
Cheetahs like the taste of sugar cane.
Leopards are like a dot-to-dot.
Jaguars are like leopards a lot.
Panthers are like a big black cat.
I would just like to say I love my cat.

Carissa Louise Shaibi-uter (10)
Hucklow Primary School

What Is Snow?

It is a white sheet covering the world,
A frozen pile of ice cream,
It is a flock of sheep running through the sky,
A cold blanket warming the earth.

Lewis Barry (10)
Hucklow Primary School

What Is The Rainbow?

In the sky
A jar of sweets spread on
the grey carpets
On a sheet.
A load of paint has been spilt
with paint pot on the white pillow.
Dropped pencil crayons on the
classroom floor.

Trelawny Brown (10)
Hucklow Primary School

What Is The Moon?

A ten pence coin shining in the vastness of space.
A white football kicked in the air
It is a silent clock hanging on a big black wall
A ball of cotton wool, big and bright.
It is a large pile of icing sugar on a black cake.
A torchlight beaming at midnight.

Amy Louise Farrell (9)
Hucklow Primary School

What Is Snow?

Snow is a white blanket.
Snow is icing sugar sprinkled on the floor.
It is thick ice cream.
A feather floating through the air.

Jahed Ahmed (10)
Hucklow Primary School

Sky Changes

The sky at sunrise is like swirled ink,
The colours are red, orange and pink.
The colours have got a calm motion,
It is just like the big blue ocean.
Sometimes the sky can be grey,
I sit on my bed and say what an awful day.
When I see the sun shine so bright,
I seem to get happier because of the light.
Sky changes.

Ashleigh Crump (11)
Hucklow Primary School

What Is A Rainbow?

A semicircle of colours
A target of colour
A multicoloured bow and arrow
A box of crayons
A flower bed of colours.

Kyle Peachey (10)
Hucklow Primary School

Respect

If you show others respect
they will respect you right back.
Respect everyone
whether they are
blue, red, white, green or black.

Don't bully people
whoever they are.
Respect people
whoever they are,
whether they come
from near or from far.

We are all from the human race.
The only thing that is not the same
is the colour of our skin.
Respect one another.
Kick racism out!

Saeed Yusuf (11)
Hucklow Primary School

What Is Wind?

A big dragon flying in the sky
Giants blowing
Gigantic fan breathing
Making tree fall
Foghorns
Extremely loud noises
A huge popped tyre.

Bilal Qasim (9)
Hucklow Primary School

Bullying

It always happens in the playground
It always happens in the loo
They wait outside the school gate
Just to pick on you.

Torment you, kick you, and call you names
Won't let you join in any games.

It happens at the bus stop
It happens in the class
They always know the right time
No adults walking past.

It always happens in the corridor
It always happens in the yard
They used to be your pals once
Now they hit you hard.

Push you, pull you, nip and squeeze
Saying cruel things, just to tease.

Take your sweets, crisps and money
Laugh at you, pretend it is funny.

It happens all the time
No one is ever there to see
What I'd like to know is
Why is it always me?

They always spy
Just to make you cry
They swear and fight
And give others a fright.

Shelina Khan (10)
Hucklow Primary School

I Love School

If you come to school
You're cool
If you don't come to school
You're a fool
Don't act crazy
Don't be lazy
Get out of bed
And fill your head
Listen to your teacher and
Don't be a silly creature
Don't make a funny feature
Do as you are told
Then you'll get a pot of gold!

Aneesa Ahmad (9)
Hucklow Primary School

Bus To School

Rounding the corner
It comes to a stay
Quick! Grab the rail
Now we're on our way . . .
Oh, but it's Thursday
The day of fear!
Three hateful lessons!
And school draws near.

Some children love school
I'd rather go to the swimming pool.
Some children are small
And some are tall.
They love to play
Then go to the classroom
And play with clay.
But I think all the kids
Like to stay.

Manal Al-Hakam (11)
Hucklow Primary School

My Mum Thinks . . .

My mum thinks that I'm asleep
but I'm eating everything in the fridge.
My mum thinks that I'm asleep
but I'm going on a bike ride.
My mum thinks that I'm asleep
but I'm going around the world.
My mum thinks that I'm asleep
but I'm going into space.
My mum thinks that I'm asleep
but I'm entering the world rally.
My mum thinks that I'm asleep
but I'm going to Paris on a million pound shopping trip.
My mum thinks that I'm asleep
but I'm on the biggest ride in the world.
My mum thinks that I'm asleep
then she wakes me up just when I'm going to be
crowned queen of the world!

Natalie Ardron (10)
Hucklow Primary School

This Is Meadowhall!

M others pushing prams round and round.
E verybody is chatting and that makes such a beautiful sound.
A ctivity is everywhere.
D ozens of people shop without a care.
O ld people keep themselves to themselves.
W hile young children look for Santa's elves.
H ow do they do this?
A Saturday they never miss.
L aughter is filling the air.
L ooking in the windows they can't help but stare.

Kyle Judge (10)
Hucklow Primary School

Eraser In My Blazer

There was a young boy called Razor
Who lost his favourite eraser
He looked everywhere
Even under his chair
And found it tucked in his blazer.

Joseph Luke Grimwood (10)
Hucklow Primary School

What Is Thunder?

Drums getting hit in the sky
1,000 horses running around the city
Doors slamming in people's houses
Bins banging in people's alleyways
Giant footsteps in Heaven
Crashing noises outside.

Amir Munir (9)
Hucklow Primary School

What Is The Moon?

A metallic football on a dark pitch
A ball of extinguished flame in the sky
A shiny button on a black leather jacket
A five pence silver coin lost in a muddy puddle
A steel drum banged by lightning in the night sky
A glowing pearl on a lonely sea.

Micah Slater-Clayton (10)
Hucklow Primary School

What Is A Moon?

A crystal rolling into a cave
A bouncy ball jumping into a swamp
A bright banana sleeping in the night
A shiny disco ball lighting up in a black ceiling
A silver button attached to a dark clock.

Sidrha Ali (10)
Hucklow Primary School

What Is Snow?

A long sheet of white paper
Wrapping itself around the city.
White teeth falling from the sky.
Blobs of ice cream stuck to buildings.
Giants dropping icing all over the world.

Bradie Modest (10)
Hucklow Primary School

The Snow

Field full with snow
A tablecloth covering a table
A snowy sea covering the world
A snow is a window
A big pile of sky, heaped up by trees
A snow blanket warming the roof
A snow is a wall.

Ali Alabbasi (9)
Hucklow Primary School

What Is Lightning?

An electric shock
A piece of cheese
A twitchy bulb that goes on and off
A piece of spaghetti falling from the sky
It is a silver dragon flying across the city.

Thomas Paredes-Lee (9)
Hucklow Primary School

What Is Snow?

Snow is little white balls surrounding the sky,
That makes a big white blanket on the ground,
A big icepop with no stick to hold,
A ginormous lump of white candyfloss settling on the ground,
It's a big white board covering the floor.

Conal Khan (10)
Hucklow Primary School

What Is The Moon?

A bowling ball on a dark and spooky alley.
A football on a cloudy pitch and very quiet.
A biscuit that everyone could eat.
The number zero in a sum.
A big five pence piece that some could nick.

Aaron Greenwood (10)
Hucklow Primary School

What Is Snow?

It is a fluffy white coat worn by a tree
It is an ice cream cone
It is a white teddy bear
It is a milky vanilla milkshake
It is a packet of marshmallows
It is the clouds of Heaven
Broken into damp pieces.

Olivia Stead (10)
Hucklow Primary School

What Is The Moon?

It's a gigantic snowball,
A jigsaw of white paper,
A target for space darts,
A white bomb waiting to explode.
It's a massive football covered in a white blanket.
It is a pale Earth far away.

Munief Mukerker (10)
Hucklow Primary School

What Is Snow?

Cold white ice cream covering the ground
White icing dropping from the sky
Snowflakes dropping on the ground with jewels.

Shumina Khan (9)
Hucklow Primary School

What Is A Rainbow?

A semicircle of colours
A different coloured world
As pictures of different colours.
A multicoloured light.
A box of fireworks.
A purple mountain.
Lots of different coloured disco lights.

It is a different coloured house
With a multicoloured mouse.
My million coloured shade clock
Has got a very big sound.

A bright box of fireworks
It is disco lights shining on the floor.
A semicircle of colours.
A million shades of paint,
Splashed across the sky.

Zain Mohammed (10)
Hucklow Primary School

What Is Snow?

Feathers floating on the floor softly,
A blanket spread along the floor,
Chalk scribbled all on the ground,
Paint dropped on the cold pavement,
Sugar spread on the road,
Ice cream across the path.

Kayleigh Ann License (10)
Hucklow Primary School

Wish Upon A Star

One day I wished upon a star
to fly around the world on a unicorn
As I lie there pretending I am dead
just thinking of a unicorn and lying on its head
Flying round the world like a super star
First I would go to Africa then I would go to Mars
and maybe I would go to Venus then America
Flying through space I would see all the stars
I saw when I was lying in my bed
I would fly past them thinking
which star was it I wished upon?

Rowan Chalmers (10)
Hucklow Primary School

My Brother Larenz

My brother Larenz is six years old,
There are stories about him that have never been told.
'Sit down now!' my mum will shout,
But Larenz just laughs and races about.
He may sound naughty and a bit of a pain,
But without him my life would not be the same.
He cheers me up when I'm feeling sad,
He makes me laugh so I don't feel bad.
He always bangs his head
On the side of our bed.
He lies all the time,
He never thinks it's a crime.
He drinks so slowly
That he feels a bit lonely.
He is sometimes a bit lazy
But he is never crazy.
Larenz is my brother
And nothing will stop me loving him.

Marvis Campbell (10)
Hucklow Primary School

Stamp Out Racism

It doesn't matter what colour you are or if you are from near or far,
We all need respect.
There are great people in every race,
It doesn't matter about the colour of your face.
We all need respect.
It's what is in the inside that is important to me,
And friends with the whole world I want to be.
Let's have respect.
Stamp out racism!

Abdulrahim Elhmayle (10)
Hucklow Primary School

Swimming

It's Saturday. Yippee!
I'm going swimming with my friends.
I call for them or they call for me,
The fun never ends.
As we walk we talk and laugh
About the things we've done.
When we get to the swimming pool
We have lots of fun.
As I dive into the pool
I land on a float,
It is the shape of an animal,
I think it's a goat.
Next we try the inflatable,
It is quite sensational!
In the deep end we dive through hoops.
Twisting and swirling loop-the-loop.
Swimming and splashing,
We hear the children shout,
Then the lifeguard shouts,
'It's time to get out.'
I can't wait until next Saturday
So I can go swimming with my friends.

Jordan Fearnley (11)
Hucklow Primary School

Me And The Sky

Once I imagined I was running in the sky,
One cloud jumped up and one cloud jumped down.
Both these clouds passed me by.
A bird flew past
And I jumped upon its back.
Then thunder roared
With a *bang* and a *crack,*
Birds surrounded us.
We did not know where to go
So the birds let me go
And left me alone.
I'm still running in the sky,
I wish I could go home.

Hassan Ramzan (11)
Hucklow Primary School

Playgrounds

We want to keep the playground clean and tidy.
We always keep the classroom clean and tidy.
In the big hall we eat our dinner
If we don't keep it clean and tidy the rubbish will stink.

Khalid Sahal (11)
Hucklow Primary School

What Is Fog?

It is a ghostly boat sailing on the calm ocean.
It is a grey blanket laying on the ground.
It is a lady's scarf laying on her neck.
It is a grey pillow laying on the bed.

Grant Priestley (10)
Hucklow Primary School

Colours

Red, white, yellow and blue,
Are these colours really true?
Purple, violet, ochre and green,
The best colours I have seen.

Colours here, colours there,
Colours, colours everywhere,
What colour do you like?

Brown, orange, scarlet and grey,
We hope you have a happy day.
Turquoise and black,
As dark as a sack.

Colours here, colours there,
Colours, colours everywhere,
What colour do you like?

Dark green, dark blue and terracotta,
If you are not ill then what is the matter?
Indigo, ultramarine and sea green,
The greatest colours there has ever been.

Colours here, colours there,
Colours, colours everywhere,
What colour do you like?

Silver, gold, black, red and brown,
These colours are all around.
Yellow, green, blue and white,
Oh what a happy sight.

Colours here, colours there,
Colours, colours everywhere,
What colour do you like?

Victoria Billam-Thorp **(11)**
Hucklow Primary School

SATs Tension

Staring at my textbook trying to take it in,
But it seems to go through one ear and out into the bin.
I'm crazy with worry; I'm a time bomb set to go,
I can't sleep at night I just rock to and fro.
I think I will do badly, can't possibly do well,
The suspense it is killing me, sweat coats me like a gel.
I'm frustrated and I'm angry, I tear up all my books,
In my SATs test tension I get some funny looks.
This is as I'm usually as calm as calm can be,
But I don't know what a solid is and can't recall history.
Failing in the practise tests, I'm going quite insane,
With this SATs test tension plaguing me again.
Bloodshot eyes and beads of sweat,
In my SATs test tension they're all I ever get.
The lead snaps in my pencil when I'm trying to revise,
It is all I can do to blink the tears from my eyes.
Now the date is nearing I'm reading books galore,
I can't remember anything, I need to learn more!
One more day until the dreaded test,
Trying to stay calm, trying to rest.
Now it's the day I'm feeling very sick,
For once my mom didn't see through that trick!

Daniel Hancock (11)
Hucklow Primary School

The Sad Snake

Does a snake know how to laugh
When it slides around in the grass?

Can it chuckle as it climbs a tree?
What a sight that would be to see.

For all I've ever heard is a hiss,
How sad is this?

Emma Broadhead (10)
Nether Green Junior School

The Box Of Wonders

(Based on 'Magic Box' by Kit Wright
I made a box for my mum and dad for Christmas
and I wrote this poem to go with it)

I will put in the box the roar of a lion,
The tail feather of a phoenix,
The touch of a unicorn's horn,
The hoof print of a centaur,
The neigh of a wild stallion.

I will put in the box the joy of Christmas,
The fire from a dragon's nostrils,
The blessing of God,
The power of love.

My box is fashioned from gold of the deepest mines,
Rubies of the finest kind,
The scales of a mermaid's tail,
Stars from the sky.

My box is made just for you
Love Imogen.

Imogen Cassels (7)
Nether Green Junior School

The Howling Wind

The howling wind makes me afraid,
I want the horrid noise to fade,
I do not want to go outside,
I want my mother, so I cried.
Dad says I'm silly,
'I think so too!' says Milly.
I hid away for ages
And the hamsters went into their cages.
All my fear is here to stay,
I can't believe it's only May!
Why won't it go away?
Why . . . ?
Why won't it go away?

Hannah Slaughter (9) & Caroline Barton (10)
Nether Green Junior School

Vikings

Although thought of as vicious raiders,
The Vikings were actually very good traders.
In the Knar (their trading ship),
They'd sell their goods on their tiring trip,
They jumped into longboats with a terrifying cry,
As they thought of the people who were going to die.
They silently sailed up the river
But had no bows or arrows or quiver.
Then with a bellow the fight was unleashed,
As the great gang of Vikings all ran up the beach.
With the terrified screams and clashing of axes,
They killed poor villagers and
Took their taxes.
Around their necks were the hammers of Thor,
Thor was the vicious and great God of war.
They all laughed at the monks retreating backs,
But killed them,
Stole their artefacts.
They took some people back as slaves
And made them row across glistening waves.
When they got back, they'd tell their tale,
Whilst slurping noisily at their ale.
Passing their stories on through the ages,
So we can read them on these pages.

Lucy Bradley (8)
Nether Green Junior School

Eagle

Diving, wheeling in the sky,
Time to hunt or I must die,
Banking, twisting, wind in my feathers,
Spot a rabbit in the heathers,
Diving, swooping, mind the gorse,
Where *is* that rabbit? I could eat a horse!

David Cousins (8) & Jennifer Cousins (11)
Nether Green Junior School

Food

What about a sandwich with honey, jam or cheese?
My favourite one is bacon on wholemeal, if you please.

Mummy likes a salad, Daddy likes a pie,
And Jess our dog, eats anything, she'll even eat a fly!

When it comes to ice cream, all kinds I like to eat
Vanilla, chocolate, strawberry, I like them as a treat.

Mummy likes Italian food, Daddy likes a curry
And Jess our dog eats super fast, as if she's in a hurry.

I'm learning in the kitchen to chop and cook our food
And learning when I'm eating, to talk and eat is rude.

And Mummy, Daddy and myself have learned to our distress
That if we do not watch our food, it all ends up in Jess!

Elliot Whiteside (8)
Nether Green Junior School

A Barn Owl When Hunting

A barn owl is like a white ghost
floating in the darkness.
The moon lights up his snowy-white feathers
as soft as silk.
His talons are ready as he swims
through the sky.
Then suddenly he plunges to the ground
like a diver in the ocean.
A second later he swoops up again,
clutching a dead mouse in his beak and glides away
Back into the darkness.

Holly Williams (10)
Nether Green Junior School

Eaglet

One fine day had dawned to see six eggs in a nest,
The next had seen, instead of eggs, six eaglets all at rest.

Five were gold as gold could be, as gold as the crown of a king,
But one was brown, as the cold brown Earth and how he loved to sing.

He would sing all day, sitting in the nest and only cease at night,
Until one day he learned to fly and sang all day in flight.

All his siblings had left the nest and were hunting for themselves,
So he flew down to dig for worms where the badger delves.

Digging for worms was such good fun, the eaglet dropped his guard,
To a hungry fox, just passing by, to catch he looked not hard.

The fox crept up until in range, to pounce upon his prey,
But the eaglet heard him creeping up and flew, far, far away.

The eaglet soon became an eagle, so elegant and grand,
So tall and proud upon a cliff, he would love to stand.

As an eagle he hunted bigger prey, like small birds, mice and voles,
Unlike the worms he used to hunt, his prey left no holes.

The eagle died a peaceful death, sleeping in his nest,
Because for him, so old and weary, rest at last was best.

Maddy Cousins (10)
Nether Green Junior School

Firework Party

On Bonfire Night we have a celebration,
Neighbours cry in exclamation!
Why make fireworks boom again?
All your money to silver rain!
They're howling like baby monkeys,
That have been pulled out of their trees!
They can complain but they have no brain!
Next year we are having one again.

Eigen Horsfield (10)
Nether Green Junior School

Like Loo!

Do you know a dog like Loo?
She is sensitive,
She is beautiful,
She is silly.

She is soft as a brush,
She is silky.

When she has had a bath she
Dries herself on the walls.

She is crazy,
She is tender,
She has a happy wagging tail.

She is our Dotty Daydream.

Sam Denton (9)
Nether Green Junior School

Homework

1, 2, 3. A, B, C - homework's
finished let's jump with glee!
Oh no, there's more,
this means war.
Heading for the door
there's loads more
23 + 8 better make a quick escape.
Next day at school, headmaster's
going to be cruel.
Detention again got 4 out of ten,
my mum's just a tad mad
my dad's an angry lad
and all because of homework!

Laura Lee (10)
Nether Green Junior School

Death

Is where your heart stops dead
like a car at a red light.
It is the time where good people
go to Heaven to live a
longer life with God.
Death is where the people
you love have to suffer as well
as the people who love you.
People will have to carry on living
life but it will never be the same.

Grace Hector (11)
Nether Green Junior School

Chocolate

Tasty, delicious, chocolate sitting in the fridge,
Just one step further and it could be mine,
Will it be as tasty as it looks?
Will my mouth water with the scrumptious taste?
I can't wait any longer . . .
Mmmm that was delicious!

Tessa Godley (10)
Nether Green Junior School

Why!

Why are there trees? Why are there bees?
Why are there hares? Why are there bears?
Why is there Mars? Why are there stars?
Why are there cats? Why are there bats?
Why is there ice? Why are there mice?
Why is there day and why is there night?

Does anybody know?

Pouyan Maleki (9)
Nether Green Junior School

The Moon

Lean your head back,
What do you see?
The twinkle of stars
Looking at me.

Then look more to the
East and look at the
Glistening moon
And look at it shining
Down on you.

How bright it becomes
As the shine of the moon
Turns into a smile
Creeping across the sky.

Then the sky starts
To lighten with green
Pink and blue, with one
Last wink and the moon
Is gone, and the sun beams
Down on you.

Serafina Body (8)
Nether Green Junior School

Spring

This is what spring brings . . .
I hear the birds tweeting in the trees.
Watch a lamb playing by some bees,
I smell the freshness of the flowers on the lawn.
I stroll past another lamb being born,
I taste the sweet taste of sugar-coated honey.
I see a rabbit with her baby bunny,
Soon spring will end and summer will begin
But spring won't always be missing,
It will appear again next year.

Isobel Stocker (10)
Nether Green Junior School

I Love The Snow

I love the snow very much
The only trouble is it doesn't stay long,
I pray and pray for snow each day,
And out with the sledge I go to play.
Making snowmen that can't come in,
Throwing snowballs, making a din.
My feet are cold, my hands are blue,
My head is warm because my hat is new.
After we've played, it's time to go in,
To sit by the fire with a warm cup of tea.
That's why I love the snow.

Stephanie Broomhead (8)
Nether Green Junior School

School

School, school gives you an education,
School, school has imagination.

Playtime, playtime it's the *best,*
Playtime, playtime you can have the rest.

Lesson time, lesson time, makes you learn,
Lesson time, lesson time, crash and burn.

Lunchtime, lunchtime, yummy, yummy food,
Lunchtime, lunchtime, sausage and egg.
Lunchtime sit on chairs,
Lunchtime is always fair.

Junior club, Junior club, lots of fun,
Junior club, Junior club, making a bun.

School play, school play, learn and learn,
School play, school play, take your turn.

Nether Green is the place to be
Read our poems and you can see!

Hannah Bateman (8)
Nether Green Junior School

Storms

Storms are like fierce lions,
Growling, day and night.
They cause terrible happenings,
Like fatal injuries or maybe even death.

Crash! Bang! Boom!
As it knocks over trees and bus stops.
The wind is hitting you in the face like a herd
Of elephants,
Lightning and thunder crashing
Down, like bombs.

Nobody knows when these terrible happenings
Will strike, or why?
As the storm comes to an end,
You're safe . . . or are you?

Aaron Messen (11)
Owston Park Primary School

Storm

The storm strikes solid,
The storm blows hard.
The storm spins furiously
The storm comes down rapidly.

The storm hates everyone,
The storm hits lightning.
The storm is always is in a bad mood,
The storm scares us with its thunder.

The storm is hard and rough,
The storm blows rapidly.
The storm spins furiously.

Matthias Paul Lambert (11)
Owston Park Primary School

Dreadfully Dying

You lay there screaming in pain,
Crying for help.
Laying on the roadside, bleeding,
No one comes to help, you're there alone!

Your eyes are closing,
Colour is fading.
Your blood-covered face is disgusting,
No cars go by, no one to help.

You start to cough,
Choking on your own saliva.
Spluttering and spitting it out,
It's nearly time, you're nearly gone.

The last few seconds are here,
It's time now!
Close your eyes
Never to be opened again.

Adam Blackburn (11)
Owston Park Primary School

Deserted Street

In the deserted street at night,
The street is pitch-black and dark,
You can only see the dark figures of the houses,
The silence is deafening,
The park is desolate,
The swings are swinging in the wind,
In the distance you can hear a faint hooting
Of an owl,
No movement at all.

Laura Purdy (10)
Owston Park Primary School

Football

Football, football is so mad,
The crowd always shouts, 'Shoot lad!'
People say football's bad.

Goal! The fans jump in the air,
Knock things over but they don't care.
The losing fans shout, 'That's not fair!'

The fans start singing, 'One-nil, one-nil!'
But the losing fans just chill.
It's a so good match because people
Are watching from the hill.

The winning fans say, 'This match is cool!'
Because their team is not acting like a fool.
The losing team are a drool.

Two-nil, the team's surely won now,
The losing fans say, 'Ciâo!'
Losing fans say, 'Our keeper's playing rubbish now!'

Two-one, they are back in the game,
Our keeper's playing lame.
But unfortunately the whistle goes
For the end of the game.

Adam Thorpe (10)
Owston Park Primary School

The Storm

The wind was whistling,
The gates opened,
The trees shook wildly
What was it? Was it a storm?

In the deserted street the wind was changing,
The gates swung to and fro.
Then suddenly hundreds of birds were flying,
Everywhere there were blackbirds, sparrows and crows.

Then the violent winds struck objects,
Cars, bins and sheds.
The bins toppled over to the ground,
And the sheds were demolished, so they were dead!

In the sky there was a sound,
Bang! Bash! Boom!
There was a flash of light in the sky,
What was it? Was the storm worse?

The streets were filled with a deafening silence,
The birds landed,
Everything was still,
The storm had ended!

Thomas Johnson (11)
Owston Park Primary School

Storm

The wind tremendously blows, to and fro,
As the thick cubes of hail drop to the sodden ground,
The thunder wakes up the sleeping town,
Whilst the lightning dazzles up the dew-covered yard.

The rain rapidly falls,
A freezing cold chill fills the air,
The wind piercing through the trees,
Red skies signify the coming dawn.

Lauren Winfield (11)
Owston Park Primary School

Where Am I?

This place is different, I'm all alone,
What to do? Where to go?
I'm scared to move, I silently wait,
I look around is this my fate?

The city I'm in silently sleeps,
Whilst my feet try to creep.
I hear a sound, I turn my head,
I close my eyes, I'm filled with dread.

In front of me stands a man,
I'll speak to him, I know I can,
I tried to shout, 'Hang on! Wait!'
But there's no point it's too late.

The next thing I see is a whirling light,
It pulls me towards it, I try to fight,
I can't hold on, I just let go,
And that was it, that's all I know.

Lorna White (11)
Owston Park Primary School

My Dad

My dad is quite tall,
He has blond hair and blue eyes,
He watches Sheffield United,
It's no big surprise,
He takes me down to The Lane
To watch the Blades play again and again.
When they win, it's a glorious time,
But when they lose, he's not just fine.
He's grumpy and sad and feels let down,
But maybe next week they'll make him smile again
Down at Bramall Lane.

Jamie Barrett (9)
Rudston Preparatory School

Bonfire Night

B angers, bang in the air
O ver they go, above our heads
N oisily children shout, everywhere
F unny fireworks, set off from the ground
I ncredible games, the children play
R ockets rising in the air
E xciting explosions fill the air.

N ight lasting longer and longer, as it goes on
I see Catherine wheels turning and turning
G lowing fireworks fill the air
H appy children, watch and listen
T onight is the night when Guy Fawkes burns.

Thomas Velamail (9)
Rudston Preparatory School

A Bonfire Night Acrostic Poem

B ang! Boom! as the fireworks explode in the night.
O pen your firework packs and the Jumping Jacks,
N o, you're not old enough! Soon you will
F lickering flames come out from the bonfire
I n the party, lots of food and drinks
R unning fast, excited children, outside
E ntertainment all through the night.

N o light, just darkness, with coloured sparklers
I n the sky. On his lonely throne, the Guy slowly burns.
G lowing till the morning light
H ave a big celebration. What a sight!
T onight is the night of all nights.

Nabeel Ahmed (9)
Rudston Preparatory School

Oh To Be A Golf Ball

I am in his hands, placed on the *tee*
I wonder what will happen to *me*
Whoosh! Whoosh, the wind whistles *by*
He's swinging the club, I could *cry*
Then all of a sudden, there's a very loud *crack*
And off I go, there's no turning *back*
Flying through the air, a hundred miles per *hour*
Where will I land, my he's got some *power*
I hit the ground and I bounce *along*
It must be good, he's singing a *song*
One more hit and along I *roll*
Then with a plop, I drop in the *hole!*

Joshua Jackson (8)
Rudston Preparatory School

Bonfire Night

B angs and flashes fill the night sky,
O range flames warm my face.
N oise of children laughing in the dark,
F ood smells coming from the barbecue.
I ndoors, my pets are safe and warm.
R ockets explode high over my head.
E verybody will remember this special night.

N obody wants the beautiful fireworks to end.
I hold my sparkler at arm's length.
G irls' shrieks are heard by all,
H igher and higher, the rockets shoot,
T onight is the best Bonfire Night of all.

Lydia Sharpe (8)
Rudston Preparatory School

Bonfire Night

B ang, boom, bang
O range fireworks light up the sky
N oisy fireworks light up in the sky
F ireworks go fizz
I ncredible flames
R ockets make a noisy sound in the sky
E ating is the best thing

N o one misses this night of fun
I ncredible flames
G lowing flames
H ot flames
T onight is the night.

Anastasia Efthymiou (8)
Rudston Preparatory School

My School

My school is very good
I especially like the Christmas pud!
My music teacher is called Mr Gyte
I think he is very bright
In Lower 1 and Lower 2 sometimes you can
Choose what you want to do
In Lower 3 and Lower 4 sometimes you have
to hold the door
In Upper 1 and Upper 2 you have to be
told what to do
In Upper 3 and Upper 4 I think they like
to go out the door
I'm in Upper 2 - so boo, boo, boo!

Brydie Adams (8)
Rudston Preparatory School

Bonfire Night Acrostic Poem

B oom bright fireworks go up and up
O ver rooftops they go
N ight is when it starts. Bonfire Night
F antastic flames from the fire
I mpressive fizzes and noises from the fireworks
R ound goes the Catherine wheel
E ating hot-dogs will keep you warm

N oisy night from the fireworks
I love Bonfire Night
G uy Fawkes is on top of the bonfire
H orses, dogs and cats should be kept inside
T onight is the best night ever.

Amy Croggon (9)
Rudston Preparatory School

Bonfire Night

B angers zoom into the sky
O ften you see them fly.
N o don't pay for food
F orever a cool dude
I am over here
R oaring for a cheer
E veryone having fun.

N obody leaving a bun
I f you want to come.
G et in and have some fun
H ooray, a lovely sight,
T oday was Bonfire Night.

Nour Assous (8)
Rudston Preparatory School

Delia's Daring Delight

Toad's green eyes, bubbling hot
With magic beans in a sizzling pot

Stir in eggs with skinny, long legs
And mix it well with your brother's hair gel.
Fry thin slices of beef
Then drop in some rotten old teeth.
Whisk in wing of bees
Then fold in a pair of knobbly knees.
Drop in a large spoonful of jam
Altogether with dices of ham
Into the oven it goes
For just as long as a dragon's toes.

Toad's green eyes, bubbling hot
With magic beans in a sizzling pot.

Alice Jones (8)
Rudston Preparatory School

Dragons

Dragons have very hot fire breath
You will have to watch out
Or you will be next
If not it might be your friend
Who will have to bend
Watch out, he is running
He might cut off your right ear
Or he might singe off your hair
So you'd better not be there!

Oliver Dennis (9)
Rudston Preparatory School

Food

Why is it? How can it be?
The things I like are bad for me
Milkshake, ice cream, sweets and cake
They're the best, for goodness sake!
Mum keeps using silly words
Additives, E-numbers, how absurd!
I don't want oat bran like a horse,
Give me more tomato sauce!
McDonald's, Wimpy, KFC
That's where I would like to be!
Fast food means I get it quicker
Mum says it makes my waistline thicker!
I know I'll have to change my ways
From chips to low fat mayonnaise!
A nice, long life would really suit
Go on, I'll try a piece of fruit!

Bradley Cutts (9)
Rudston Preparatory School

Electricity

Electricity comes in wires
Electricity causes fires,
Electricity makes the house live,
Electricity lets me watch Channel Five,
Electricity makes my toast,
Electricity, I like the most.

Electricity powers my PS2
It powers my Scalextrics too.
Watch out for pylons' deadly shocks,
It would help if you wore rubber socks.
Dad has an electric friend which makes nice bread,
Mum's electric blanket warms their bed.

George Daly (9)
Rudston Preparatory School

My Dad

My dad is clever, my dad is smart
We always have a very big lark
My dad is tough, my dad is cool
But sometimes he acts like a fool
He is fit, he is strong
He always wears a *frilly thong!*
He sometimes gets mad
But I still love my dad!

Thomas Henderson (9)
Rudston Preparatory School

The Jabberwocky
(Inspired by 'Jabberwocky' by Lewis Carroll)

I hear a rumble, what could it be?
Something must be following me!
Is it a bird? Is it a snake? Is it something
I can take? There it is in front of me -
The Jabberwocky!

Sarra Murphy (11)
Thurgoland CE Primary School

Macbeth

M acbeth doth murder sleep,
A very nervous man.
C ruel old lady Macbeth,
B ad Macbeth killed his own nephew,
E nters out of room with two bloodstained daggers
T oo afraid to face what has happened
H ere it ends.

Hayley Hewitt (10)
Thurgoland CE Primary School

Witches' Spell

A kangaroo's toe,
A lion's foe.
A pair of piranhas,
And some mouldy bananas.
A parrot's tail
An ogre's nail.
A human thumb
And a baboon's bum.
A devil's horn
And a baby just born.
Now that we have brewed this spell,
Let us send it down to Hell.

Matthew Waterhouse (11)
Thurgoland CE Primary School

Panic

Panic sucks at my soul
creating a gaping hole
with my breath pushed out of me.
down I fall -
to eternity.

My shock holds me still,
my body running a fire drill.
I can't move at all
as if all around me -
a giant wall.

I try to lift my legs,
but find them stuck down by invisible pegs.
I didn't plan it,
being sucked at -
by panic.

Simon Rodley (10)
Thurgoland CE Primary School

Rugby World Cup 2003

Out to the pitch came England,
Rising from their seats were the crowd.
The first-half whistle blew to start the game
And the fans sang out aloud.

Australia scored the first try,
England - nil : Australia - five.
Then Jonny Wilkinson scored a conversion
And the game came alive.

Then the score got scary,
A tie of seventeen-all.
But England really wanted to win,
So England were on Australia like a big, brick wall.

Then Jonny Wilkinson scored a blasting kick,
Through the two giant metal bars it flew.
England celebrated the score of twenty-seventeen,
And then the final whistle blew.

Then that golden man, Jonny Wilkinson,
Showed his glory and fame.
He held up the shining rugby World Cup,
It had been the greatest rugby World Cup game.

Greg Holmes (10)
Thurgoland CE Primary School

Universe

Swirling, twirling Milky Way,
There's no air up there, you could die.
Sleepy darkness is here to stay,
Way up in the sky.

The bright sun lights up the Earth,
A rocket is going to the moon.
A star is being pictured at birth,
Goodbye Earthlings, come back soon!

Gabbi St Matthew-Daniel (10)
Thurgoland CE Primary School

The Big Bad Witch

In a deep, dark cave, a witch was making a spell with . . .
Guinea pig's blood
Cows' ears
Rabbit food
Snakes' tongue
Sheep's wool
Horses' lips
A mouldy apple
Sharks' teeth
Human skin
Cats' toenails
Sticky red jam
Baboon's blood to cool it down
All mixed together to make children behave
Like they should.

Alice Dodd (10)
Thurgoland CE Primary School

Tickle Or Prickle?

Hedgehogs prickle
Spiders tickle
Rabbits bounce
Lions pounce

Penguins slide
Eagles glide
Mice squeak
Crickets creak

Horses neigh
Cats play
Elephants stomp
Tigers chomp.

Adam Dewsnap (11)
Thurgoland CE Primary School

What's Going On In The Playground?

What's going on in the playground?
Children laugh and children cry,
Noise deafens the teachers
Who are slowly passing by.
What's going on in the playground?

What's going on in the playground?
Girls all chitter and chatter,
The boys were playing football
But their ball's now in the gutter.
What's going on in the playground?

What's going on in the playground?
'Argh! I've hurt my leg!'
'Jamie and Connor are fighting, Miss,'
'Can I go for a wee?' we beg.
What's going on in the playground?

What's going on in the playground?
Everybody's marching indoors.
The bell has just been rung
Let's see what playtime has caused,
What's going on in the playground?

What's going on in the playground?
Nothing . . . *until!*
What's going on in the playground?

Bethany Dobbin (11)
Thurgoland CE Primary School

My Alphabet Of Friends

A shleigh likes to make a noise,
B ethany always plays with boys.
C harlie likes to make a fuss,
D aniel likes it on the bus,
E lliot likes to play football.
F rankie can't play sports at all,
G reg likes drawing, he's the best,
H aley likes to make a mess,
I ssy goes gymnastics crazy.
J oseph though, is rather lazy.
K athy likes to read a book,
L iam likes to roll in muck,
M atthew likes to watch TV,
N icky eats baked beans for tea.
O llie likes to have a bath,
P aula likes to have a laugh.
Q uamay likes to go on walks,
R ebecca likes to chat and talk,
S imon wants to be a vet
T anya likes the Internet.
U rsula likes to roller-skate,
V icky's almost always late!
W alter likes to play CDs
X ara's cat is full of fleas,
Y vonne likes to sing and dance,
Z ack is into trees and plants.

All these people are my friends,
I hope our friendship never ends!

Hannah Newbery (11)
Thurgoland CE Primary School

The Hobbit

(Based on 'The Hobbit' by J R R Tolkien)

Once upon a time, there was a hobbit his name was Bilbo Baggins
He did nothing interesting, was not very bling-bling

But then some dwarves came huddling in
Then Gandalf appeared with a rather large grin.
He told him about a quest and then about a pot of gold
The hobbit hurried off outside, even though it was terribly cold.

Lots of dwarves and Gandalf too, Bilbo Baggins joins the crew,
So they set off, about twenty-two
But what they got into, they didn't have a clue!

Battled Orcs through the wood
Goblins, trolls, they paid for with blood.
Icy mountains, murky trails
Lots of monsters on their tails.

At last they reached the cave of gold
But they didn't know what lay beyond,
Bilbo went into the cave but when he saw that dragon sleeping
And saw the treasure underneath, he decided to go in creeping.

He felt the treasure in his grasp
But then the dragon woke, with a massive roar of smoke.
Unleashing its frustration on the nearest town it could find
But the town was prepared and the dragon attacked up -
Down and behind.

There were swords flying, arrows zooming,
The dragon, named Smaug, rampage was booming,
With jewels and diamonds on its golden belly,
Destroying the town like it was jelly.

But then the dragon perched itself on the bridge,
Where Gandalf pulled off a magic trick and the bridge fell to pieces
As the dragon sank with a horrifying *puff!*

The dragon was slayed, the party begun
Their quest was repaid, it was time for fun!

Joey Brayford (11)
Thurgoland CE Primary School

If
(Based on 'If' by Rudyard Kipling)

If you can be lied about and not retaliate
If you can be laughed at and can take the joke
If you can share something about yourself and not exaggerate
If you can be treated badly and you are not provoked

If you can recognise your faults and have the will to change
If you can love and not be loved
If you can be brave when others are in danger
If you can be poor and still be happy

If you can hear rumours and not believe in them
If you can be doubted, yet still have the strength to carry on
If you can be rich and share with the poor
Then your new life has just begun.

Rhys Kyte (11)
Tickhill St Mary's CE Primary & Nursery School

Your Life Ahead
(Based on 'If' by Rudyard Kipling)

If you can be rich and share with the poor
If you can be kind and not break the law
If you can be laughed at and take the joke
If you go blind and still have some hope

If you can be clever and not show off
If you can be fine not doing a millionaire cough
If you can be scared but yet be brave
If you can be friendly and try to behave
Then your new life has just begun
And you'll do well, my son.

Michael Hunter (10)
Tickhill St Mary's CE Primary & Nursery School

Advice In Life

(Based on 'If' by Rudyard Kipling)

If you hear rumours and don't believe them,
If you tell the truth and not lie,
If you can make decisions and know when
If you can budget but still buy,

If you can have fun but don't go wild,
If you change but still be the same,
If you can act calmly but not too mild,
If you can make choices yet keep to your aim,

If you can be helpful but not too much,
If you can be sensible but not be too wise,
If you can be fair and still get lucky,
If you can have less enemies and not be despised,

If you can have a family and be loved,
If you can be liked and not be tricked,
If you can be brave and not get shoved,
If you can do all this then it has clicked.

Tui Krösschell (10)
Tickhill St Mary's CE Primary & Nursery School

A New Beginning

(Based on 'If' by Rudyard Kipling)

If you can be laughed at and laugh with them,
If you can be doubted but still have the strength to carry on,
If you can hear rumours and don't believe in them,
If you can be rich but share with the poor,

If one bad thing happens, don't give up on everything.
If you can recognise your faults and have the will to change,
If you could meet with success and not brag or show off,
If you can be scared but be brave when it is needed,
If you can love and not be loved back,
If you can be poor but still be happy,
Then you will have success in becoming an adult.

Georgia Ashton (10)
Tickhill St Mary's CE Primary & Nursery School

A Poem That Will Change Your Life

(Based on 'If' by Rudyard Kipling)

If you can be lied about and not retaliate
If you can hear rumours and don't believe them
If you can meet with success and don't show off
If you can be yourself in every situation
If you can accept the bad things as they come
If you don't tell secrets about your friends

If you can love and not be loved
If you can be poor and still be happy
If you can be laughed at and take the joke
If you can be rich and share with the poor
If you can recognise your faults
And have the will to change

If you can be scared and get to be brave
If you can be doubled up yet still have strength to carry on
If you can dream and not make dreams your life
If you can be sad inside and still be happy on the outside

If you see a fight and don't get involved
If you lose a race and are not a bad loser
If you can keep your feelings all locked up
If you can have a job and still have time for family

If you can speak the truth and take the consequences
If you lose all your money then start again at the beginning
And never breathe a word of your fall
Then you will become close to becoming perfect.

Holly Parker (11)
Tickhill St Mary's CE Primary & Nursery School

Change
(Based on 'If' by Rudyard Kipling)

If you can be hated but not hate back
If you can be scared yet still be brave
If you can be laughed at and still take the joke
If you can be rich but share with the poor

If you an be yourself in every situation
If you can be lied about yet not retaliate
If you hear rumours yet do not believe in them
If you can recognise your faults and have the will to change

If you can love and not be loved
If you can meet with success and not show off
If you can be poor but still be happy
Then your new life has just begun.

Emily Sidebottom (9)
Tickhill St Mary's CE Primary & Nursery School

Perfect Person
(Based on 'If' by Rudyard Kipling)

If you can face evil and still succeed
If you have lots but can still share
If you believe, never give up
If you can be hopeful with no guarantee,

If you can be happy, liking everyone,
If harm is done forgive and forget
If you long for others' presence although they're gone
If you can do well and not expect attention,

If you can be knowledgeable and still have friends
If you put others before yourself
And if you care for all living things
You will accomplish many things.

Rebecca Wells (11)
Tickhill St Mary's CE Primary & Nursery School

If

(Based on 'If' by Rudyard Kipling)

If you can be laughed at and take the joke
If you hear rumours don't believe in them
If one bad thing happens, don't give up
Just keep trying
Otherwise you'll be unpopular.

If happy, carry on being happy
If you lose a game and are sad
Don't be a sore loser
If you're stuck with your work
Build up the work and carry on.

If you can recognise your faults
You have to change them
If you're bored change your mind
If you can meet with success and not show off
If you do you will be popular
If you are happy and still work hard
You will get a good job.
If you are rich, give to the poor
And make them happy, you'll be popular
Then your new life's just begun.

Peter Evison (10)
Tickhill St Mary's CE Primary & Nursery School

At The Seaside

One by one
We lay in the sun
Two by two
We build sandcastles
Helped by Auntie Sue
Three by three
We fish in the sea
Four by four
We knock on the fisherman's door
We had so much fun!

Eliza Harman (8)
Tickhill St Mary's CE Primary & Nursery School

Life Of Rules

(Based on 'If' by Rudyard Kipling)

If you could love but not be loved,
If you could be rich but not be touched,
If you could be laughed at and take the joke,
If you could hurt but not provoke.

If you could be poor but still be joyful,
If you could be tough but still emotional,
If you could be greedy and share with others,
If you could be hateful, love your brothers.

If you could have doubts but still go along,
If you could carry on when you know you are wrong,
If you have a poor life but still have fun,
Then it's true new life has just begun.

Daniel Donnelly (10)
Tickhill St Mary's CE Primary & Nursery School

The Way You Should Be

(Based on 'If' by Rudyard Kipling)

If you can be sad inside but remain happy on the outside,
If you can hate someone but not show it,
If you can have dinner with the queen
But still have fish and chips with your family,
If you can lose an important competition
But not be sour for the rest of your life,
If you can live under another man's shadow and still shine,
If you can really want something but not steal it,
If you can do a good thing but not brag for the rest of your life,
If you can risk your life for loved ones,
If you can buy a Porsche but not show it off,
If you can lose a loved one and not be sour to others,
This is the way *we all* should be.

Ben Carter (10)
Tickhill St Mary's CE Primary & Nursery School

Your New Life

(Based on 'If' by Rudyard Kipling)

If you could not fight even when provoked,
If you could be laughed at and still take the joke,
If you could get on without being shoved,
If you could love and not be loved,
If you could be rich and give to the poor,
If you could lose and not be sore,
If you could win and be a good sportsman,
If you could help and do the best you can,
If you can do all that I have done,
Then your new life has just begun.

Josiah Brown (10)
Tickhill St Mary's CE Primary & Nursery School

If

(Based on 'If' by Rudyard Kipling)

If you can be poor and still be happy,
If you can be terrified and still hang on,
If you can be rich and share with the poor,
If you can be scared but be brave for someone,

If you can love but not be loved,
If you can deal with sadness and still be happy,
If you can be angry and not let it blow,
Then you can be proud and not be slow.

If you can be laughed at and still take the joke,
If you can be small and still do good things,
If you can deal with things that are big,
If you can recognise your faults and change them,
If you can be lied about and not retaliate,
If you can share and not argue,
If you can be yourself in every situation,
Then you are a very successful person my friend.

Stephanie Clark (10)
Tickhill St Mary's CE Primary & Nursery School

Rules Of Life

(Based on 'If' by Rudyard Kipling)

If you can be yourself in every situation,
If you can love but not be loved,
If you can hear rumours and not believe in them,
Then you will have success in life.

If you can be rich but give to the poor,
If you can recognise your mistakes and have the will to change,
If you can be doubted but still carry on,
Then you will have success in life.

If you can be laughed at and take the joke,
If you can meet with success and not brag,
If you are scared but can be brave for someone in danger.
Then you will have success in life.

Joshua Oldham (10)
Tickhill St Mary's CE Primary & Nursery School

T-Rex

The king of the dinosaurs
Ferocious with big, sharp claws
They stomp through the trees
Do anything they please

Loud as the wind they growl
The sound is scary and foul
They stare with eyes so black
The frightened animals stare back

With sharp, pointy teeth they tear
The other dinosaurs must beware
When I go to the woods to play,
I'm pleased T-rex doesn't live today.

Holly Jackson (8)
Tickhill St Mary's CE Primary & Nursery School

A Swish Of A Silky Summer Day

Baby-blue sky,
Fluffy cotton clouds,
Yellow, fiery sun,
Pink, pretty chrysanthemums,
Newly cut grass,

Powdery beige sand,
Crystal clear sea,
Icy blue sea,
Green, smooth seaweed,
Tall, sturdy sandcastles,

Everlasting school holidays,
Warm, friendly holidays,
Large stone cottages,
Bobbing blue ferries,
Silver, streamlined aeroplanes.
Bursting, packed cars.

Red baby squirrels,
Glossy baby horses,
Chocolate baby rabbits,
Ginger baby foxes,
Striped baby badgers,
Grey baby hares,

Red and purple pansies,
Yellow-brown sunflowers,
Red, rosy poppies,
Orange, golden marigolds,
Blue-yellow hyacinths,

Georgiana Oldham (8)
Tickhill St Mary's CE Primary & Nursery School

My Pet Dog

My pet dog eats a lot of meat
And sleeps in a heap
Tries not to make a peep

My pet dog has lots of toys
Makes a lot of noise
Loves to play with boys

My pet dog likes to play in the park
It makes him bark
But he doesn't like the dark.

Zack Levers (9)
Tickhill St Mary's CE Primary & Nursery School

Your New Life Is Ahead Of You

(Based on 'If' by Rudyard Kipling)

If you can be lucky, don't show off,
If you can be scared but be brave for someone in danger,
If you can be rich share with the poor, or you'll be unpopular;

If you can be famous, still be yourself,
If you can be poor and still be happy,
If you are bad, have the will to change, or you'll be unpopular;

If you are kind, carry on being kind,
If you can hear rumours, don't believe them
If you can, love and be loved, or you'll be unpopular;

If you can be clever and still work hard,
If you can be doubted, yet still have the strength to carry on,
If you don't help you can change,
Then your new life has just begun.

Natasha Jewison (10)
Tickhill St Mary's CE Primary & Nursery School

A New Beginning

(Based on 'If' by Rudyard Kipling)

If you can be lied about and not retaliate
If you can be picked on and not be provoked
If you hear something about you and don't exaggerate
If you can be laughed at and take the joke

If you can always be yourself in any situation
If you are rich but share with the poor
If you don't try and ruin things with any complication
If you stand by the truth and do only by the law

If you get angry but don't go over the line
If you are scared but can still be brave
If you can be clever and not too wise
If you can see others doing better without feeling sad
If so, you'll be proud of yourself and others too.

Zoe Walters (11)
Tickhill St Mary's CE Primary & Nursery School

For A Good Life

(Based on 'If' by Rudyard Kipling)

If you can be rich and give to the poor,
If you can be poor and still give money,
If you can be ill and still hope for a cure,
If you can be laughed at and find it funny,

If you can be poor and enjoy your time,
If you can manage not to fight,
If your life is at a low and you can get it to climb,
If you can always see the light,

If you can care to change your wrong,
If you can be doubted but still succeed,
If you can get through when times are tough,
If you can believe my heart will bleed
And you will be a man my son.

Matthew Day (10)
Tickhill St Mary's CE Primary & Nursery School

The Leaky Puppy

Fast asleep and calm, the puppy on his mat.
In from school a child comes in and scoops him on her lap.
'Oh, my goodness, what can this wet be?'
The little puppy has had a . . . *wee!*

'Silly girl!' said my mummy
'You should not hold him by his tummy.'
'I only meant to give him a cuddle,
But all I've got is a great big . . . *puddle!'*

Jodie Leigh Hide (7)
Tickhill St Mary's CE Primary & Nursery School

Garden

The tall, wide trees
The buzzing, small bees.

The long grass on the lawn
The spiky green thorn.

The yellow, short grass
The people pass.

The orange, long flower
That always needs a shower.

Christopher Marsden (8)
Tickhill St Mary's CE Primary & Nursery School

Beauty The Horse

Beauty is a soft, kind horse who always likes to play
And if you look at her tail it always goes sway, sway, sway
She always likes to play in her field where it is nice and green
And if you look at her she likes to sweetly scream, scream, scream.

Tahla Krösschell (7)
Tickhill St Mary's CE Primary & Nursery School

Second World War

Hitler was behind it all
He made the population fall
A war was his plan
He was a violent man
That was the Second World War.

Kirsty Marsden (10)
Tickhill St Mary's CE Primary & Nursery School

I Wish

I wish I could fly,
Ever so high,
Higher than a plane,
A bird or a crane.

Then I could see
The whole world beneath me,
Cities, towns and streams,
People's hopes, wishes and dreams.

I wish I had the power
To build an Eiffel Tower,
To rule the world,
Help love when it's curled.

Then I could help
A dog when it yelps,
Someone when they're stuck
And animals like ducks.

Those are my wishes which can only come true,
If a miracle comes
To me and to you!

Leah Brown (9)
Tickhill St Mary's CE Primary & Nursery School

My Pet Cat

My pet cat,
Eats lots of fish
And clears the dish.

My pet cat
Hears a sound
And jumps up and around.

My pet cat
Sleeps in a heap
Opens one eye to have a peep.

John Baines (8)
Tickhill St Mary's CE Primary & Nursery School

Dragons

With a roar and a groan,
he sits alone.
With his gem and his stone,
to a dragonologist he is known,
face to face he shall be shown.

He sits in his cave
or near the mighty sea's wave.
In deep woods we find his grave,
we are the only ones their existence can save.

All good dragons need a friend,
With our help, their lives will never end.
They have the power to heal and mend,
if your heart is broken, their love will tend.

I love dragons and so will you,
after you've read this,
to you dragons are true.

Tessa Allen (10)
Tickhill St Mary's CE Primary & Nursery School

If

(Based on 'If' by Rudyard Kipling)

If you can be bullied and not bully,
If you can promise and keep the secret,
If you can give and not take,
You'll be a sensible grown-up.

If you can love but not be loved,
If you can be nice through bad times,
If you can have but not want too much,
You'll soon grow up to be mature.

If you can be hated and not retaliate,
If you can dream and not exaggerate,
If you can hope, build it up,
You'll soon be sensible my child.

Joanne Verity (11)
Tickhill St Mary's CE Primary & Nursery School

Sisters

Sisters big and sisters small,
Sisters short and sisters tall.

Sisters bossy and sisters good,
Teacher's pet and they do what they should.

Sisters bad, sisters mean,
They make you not want to be seen.

Sisters are nice, sisters play games;
But then they change and call you names.

I should know because I've got one
And if you see her you'll be gone!

You're lucky that I'm alive,
But don't worry I'll survive!

Abigail Ametewee (10)
Tickhill St Mary's CE Primary & Nursery School

Life

(Based on 'If' by Rudyard Kipling)

If you can be laughed at and take the joke
If you can be clever and don't murder or smoke
If you can be rich and share with the poor
If you can have money and not want more.

If you can meet with success and not show off
If you can be clever and not do the millionaire cough
If you can be loved and still be kind
If you can have an imaginative mind.

If you can be scared but yet be brave
If you can wait to meet your grave
If you can be bored but still have fun
Then your life has just begun.

Andrew Cotton (10)
Tickhill St Mary's CE Primary & Nursery School

Plants

See the lovely purple heather
Standing tall like a feather
See the pretty little violet
Shades of purple, indigo and lilac
See the scarlet-red rose
Busy butterfly comes and goes.

Francesca Hopkin (7)
Tickhill St Mary's CE Primary & Nursery School

Snow

S now is falling off the tree
N ow we can build a snowman
O utside
W e're having a snowball fight
M ake a snowman outside
A snowman outside in the garden
N ow it's time for it to melt.

Thomas Fritchley (7)
Toll Bar Primary School

Anger

I feel like a bus is coming at me at 1,000 miles per hour.
My temper is like a boiling kettle.
My brain is going to bubble like a spaceship
exploding into the midnight sky.
My face is turning into a rainbow of colours
rotating through my brain.
I can't stop myself I shouted like an
infuriated buffalo stomping across the plain.

Gavin Frost (11)
Toll Bar Primary School

Anger

A tormenting feeling rushing through my body
Heart's squeezing in,
A screw drilling my brain.
Help me!
Losing control of myself,
Frustrated,
Colours of warning, red, black,
Steam roaring through my ears.
Thirsty, hungry, angry
Lungs not helping, out of breath.
Temper taking over,
Anger, anger, *anger!*
Is all I think of
Mum, Dad, Mum, Dad, where are you?
I start to crumble.

Elizabeth Taylor (11)
Toll Bar Primary School

Excitement

My brain was popping and raring to go
Couldn't wait for that time of day
My body full with excitement
Making me more alive each day
I need to roar out, to calm down
I needed to do that thing
I've got to go
The suspense is too much
So much excitement, I forgot what I was doing.

Katie Robinson (10)
Toll Bar Primary School

Anger

Anger flowing through my head
A tingle running through my body making me want to burst
I clench my fists it makes me want to punch something or someone
My veins stick out of my neck
I feel like I want to smack my head on the wall
I throw my things across the room
My face turns flaming-red, then black as coal
And as dark as a purple prune
I stop and think hard about it, was it worth it?

Chelsea Fletcher (11)
Toll Bar Primary School

Anger

Anger all around me,
Burning fire beneath,
Smoke shooting out my nose,
My hair just went red,
My temper has exploded like a volcano,
Darts are hitting my heart,
A speeding train has blown my head off,
I feel like I'm spinning around in an earthquake,
My brain is popping out my ears and eyes,
My eyeballs are dangling out of my eye sockets.

Samuel Danby (11)
Toll Bar Primary School

Snowflakes

S nowy snowflakes
N ature covered in snow
O verflowing snow on the treetops
W aiting for more snow to come and fall.
F ootprints in the snow
L earning to ice skate
A lways cold when it snows
K icking snow everywhere
E xcited when I see snow
S now angels on the ground.

Jessica Job (8)
Toll Bar Primary School

Snowflakes

S now covers the ground
N othing is coloured
O ut in the cold, slippy snow
W ater under ice,
F lames keeping people warm
L ots of ice on roads
A nimals hibernating
K illing plants
E lectricity down
S now all over town.

Faran Hamblett (7)
Toll Bar Primary School

Snowing

S now is falling
N ow the ground is covered in snow
O utside is white snow
W inter has arrived
I nside is warm
N ow it is snowing even more
G reat, here comes fun, snow is good.

Laura Nicholas (6)
Toll Bar Primary School

Snowman

S nowman on the snow-white carpet
N asty blizzard blowing the snow
O ut in the coldest snow
W arm inside the house
M ighty freezing outside
A snowman stands smiling in the cold
N ow it's time for a snowball fight.

Nicky Harvey (8)
Toll Bar Primary School

Snowflakes

S now on the ground
N asty ice in the snow
O utside in the cold
W anting the snow to go away
F loating icicles in the air
L oads of snow coming down
A s snowflakes fall
K icking snow down the street
E scaping from the snow
S nowflakes on the ground.

Jade Ball (8)
Toll Bar Primary School

In The Time Of The Unicorn

Who sings the legend?
The snow falling on the treetops
The feathers of a bird
The beak of an eagle
The flowing stream
The footprints of a lion.

Where can we read it?
In the cave of a mouse
In a leaf of a bush
In a shadow of a forest
In the free world.

How shall we keep it?
The voice of a child
In the shimmer of a star
In the deep blue sea
In the long green grass.

How will we tell it?
The bark of a dog
The yelling of a baby
The miaowing of a cat
The chirping of a bird.

Jade Deere (10)
Toll Bar Primary School

Snowman

S now is falling
N ew snow is falling on the ground
O ut on the coldest day
W ind blowing into drifts
M ore snowflakes fall
A s the snow clears away
N ow everything is clear again.

Tom Chudley (8)
Toll Bar Primary School

Snowflakes

S now is icy,
N asty blizzards,
O utside everything is white,
W inter is cold when it snows,
F ootprints when you stand up,
L ots of snow has fallen,
A ll the ground is white,
K icking in the snow with your wellies on,
E ight snowmen standing still,
S nowmen melt when it rains.

Danielle Caudwell (8)
Toll Bar Primary School

Snowing

S now is falling
N ights are cold
O wls hooting
W ind blowing
I n the sky snow clouds coming
N ights are cold
G ames in the snow.

Nathan Didcott (8)
Toll Bar Primary School

Anger

Anger running through my head,
My eyes are going to pop out.
Black steam coming out my ears like a speeding train,
My face is going inky-black, sky-blue, plum-purple.
My hands crunch up as if I'm going to punch someone.
Bang, boom. It has stopped.

Lauren Butler (11)
Toll Bar Primary School

Snowflakes

S now floating in the sky
N ow snow's falling in wintertime
O h a snowflake in the sky
W hat a snowflake!
F alling from the sky, a snowflake
L eaking drips in the sky
A ll the snowflakes fall softly down
K eeping snowballs all the time
E ating pudding to keep warm
S now is falling from the sky.

Declan Fluin (6)
Toll Bar Primary School

Anger

My ears are steaming like a cooker burning dinner.
My eyes are going red like a shiny red apple,
I feel like banging my head on the table,
My whole body's going scarlet,
My eyes can only see crimson.
My head feels like it's going to explode,
My body is full of anger,
I feel I want to hit someone,
I'm losing control,
I feel I'm going to turn into the Incredible Hulk
Or even worse!

Martin Crosby (11)
Toll Bar Primary School

Snow

Snow is fun,
Snowflakes falling,
Playing in the snow,
Snow is fun.

Snowman standing on the ground,
We are running round and round,
Snow is fun.

Charlotte Bacon (7)
Toll Bar Primary School

Shay - Kenning

Good reader
Nice smiler
Chocolate eater
Clothes buyer
Good footballer.

Harry Woodward (7)
Wath Central Junior School

Metaphorical Me

I am a vicious dog,

My legs are wooden baseball bats,
My arms are bent branches,
My voice is lots of squeaky rats,
My eyes are purring black cats,
My hair is a bulging bird's nest,
My toes are straight bananas,
My ears are pointed pens,
My chest is a hairy gorilla,
My cheeks are big hens.

Matthew Leyland (10)
Wath Central Junior School

The Prisoner

Looking through the moonlit bars,
It is a dark and dreary day,
Sleeping on a bed of hay,
Lurking shadows coming closer,
My skin is rotting, getting worse.

I am as hungry as a bear stumbling, stumbling and falling.
Wet as rain crashing in the moonlit sky,
I only told a little lie!
Cold as wet slush coming to my knee,
Hungry as a lonely tramp, lonely as can be.

I feel like I'm in a cramped square,
I don't even think of what I wear.
Tiny as a black flea biting at my hairy skin,
Dejected as a lonely stray dog not allowed in.

Here he comes not so nice
Another prisoner thrown in for his vice.
'Help,' I say,
I do not want to end this way.

Megan Rees (9)
Wath Central Junior School

The Prisoner

I am as cold as snow on a damp surface
I am a hurt tree in its own lonely forest
My eyes are holes of despair,
Stranded on a rock in the sea.
I am a starving beggar, in the cold streets.
My hands are rusty metal hanging off a dark, dusty wall.
The rats are my only company in this cell
I am a gloomy ghost in an abandoned house.
I am as dirty as mud in a damp forest.
Will I ever escape this hell?

Jasmin Oxer (9)
Wath Central Junior School

The Prisoner

I am as bruised as a dropped apple on the rotten floor,
My legs are shivering like an abandoned polar bear cub,
I am as miserable as a dying man on the cold stone,
My wrists are in intolerable agony,
I am as torn as a battered boar ready for the chop,
My fingers are being demolished by frostbite,
I am furious, like a raging bull being attacked by fearless knights,
My eyes are slowly closing,
I am as decayed as an old, dreary tortoise stone-still
                                        on the gravelled ground,
My feet are glued to the old boring floor,
I am as annoyed as a man betrayed by his best friend,
My stomach is groaning at me for evermore,
Desperately crawling out with my blunt nails,
My teeth never stop chattering,
The guard's echo is getting nearer and nearer . . .
This is a living *hell*.

Sam Drury (10)
Wath Central Junior School

The Prisoner

Monstrous moving shadows, always on the wall,
I'm as cold as a snowman shivering all day long.
Injured, wounded body, bruised and hurting like a battered deer.
The dirty, tight shackles have captured my wrists,
Like a python not letting go.
I'm miserable like a rainy day, dark and gloomy.
Rotting teeth, plaque and a scruffy stench staying in the same place.
My body is like a scruffy rat, eating the scraps of food,
The Lord's scraps, in one corner making me sick.
My clothes are as soggy as a river, streaming down a waterfall.
The rats disease will come to me,
Faster than I can get out of here . . . *help!*

Matthew Elliss (9)
Wath Central Junior School

What Is Red?

Mouth-watering cherries on a bush,
Revolting, thick blood coming with a flush.

Sweet, juicy apple in a bowl,
Round, hard ball kicked in goal.

Strawberries melting in my mouth,
Shiny car, heading south.

Hard, light cups filled with tea inside,
Two hairy caterpillars, side by side.

Three beautiful flowers in a pot,
That horrible pen it makes quite a blot.

Red is lots of things!

Jack Hobson (9)
Wath Central Junior School

Metaphorical Me

I am a sporty cheetah,
My smile is a pink banana,
My eyes are brown bullets,
My voice is a fluttering butterfly,
My hair is a mass of green seaweed,
My laugh is a white sheep's baa baa,
My nose is a juicy, red strawberry,
My hands are baby octopus,
My feet are blue flowers.

Victoria Hammond (10)
Wath Central Junior School

Metaphorical Me

I am a cheeky tiger cub,
My hair is straggly noodles,
My eyes are shiny green marbles,
My smile is a sour strawberry,
My teeth are polar bear's fur,
My hands are eggs with sizzling sausage fingers,
My feet are apple trees,
My body is a large choccy finger,
I'm just metaphorical me!

Holly Fisher (10)
Wath Central Junior School

The Prisoner

I am as lonely a spider in a desert,
No one to talk to,
I am bleeding like a dead soldier fresh from battle,
The walls are crawling with rats,
The only thing I can eat,
I am bruised like a robbed traveller scared to come outside,
I am an unwell pirate with scurvy plague and more,
The rusty shackles are cutting my wrists,
My only friend is Fred, the skeleton,
I am a stinky tramp covered with dirt and insects,
I am a miserable crab crawling around,
Straw for my bed is ripping away
And the rats are biting me bad,
I am like a poor beggar pleading for food,
But . . . I didn't steal the bread!

William Campbell (9)
Wath Central Junior School

The Prisoner

I am an old, grumpy, stray dog
staring at the shiny moon,
my eyes are dull caves as dark as space,
I am as cold as icy wind
blowing through the freezing, rusty bars.
My fingers are stiff twigs, scratching
and scraping at the dirty cell walls.
I am like a rough, battered stone
the deep ocean beats against.
My voice is a black hole
screeching out like a breeze
through the cracks in the rotten walls.
I hate this hell,
will I ever escape the Lord's clutches?

Jake Blunt (9)
Wath Central Junior School

Metaphorical Me

I am a cute koala,
My head is a softy teddy bear,
My eyes are juicy oranges,
My voice is a graceful swan,
My laugh is a giggling hyena,
My hair is wriggling spaghetti,
My hands are leaves gliding from a tree,
My feet are beautiful baby dolphins,
My nose is a curled up hedgehog.

Katie Johnson (10)
Wath Central Junior School

The Animal World

Dirty dogs.
Bad bears.
Bubbling, busy bats.
Cute and cuddly cats.
Battling badgers.
Leaping lambs.
Clumsy cats.
Noisy nightingale.
Running rabbits.
Hot hamsters.
Fat frogs.
Funky foxes.
Groovy geese.
Falling fish.
Slimy snakes.

Hannah Mattingley (7)
Wath Central Junior School

All About Animals Alliteration

Entertaining elephants
Balancing bulls
Rotten rats
Greedy goats
Naughty nightingales
Vanishing voles
Wiggling worms
Talking turtles
Dancing dogs
Swimming swans
Dirty ducks
Fussy fishes
Fat frogs
Bad birds
Hurt horses.

Chloe Williams (8)
Wath Central Junior School

Wildlife Alliteration

Looping leaping leopards
Funky fish
Creeping crocodile
Cute, cuddly cats
Creeping crawling caterpillars
Diving dancing dolphins
Pouncing puppy
Karaoke kangaroo
Hairy hare.

Ellie Mae Wood (8)
Wath Central Junior School

Mrs Heaton Kenning

Nice teacher
Story teller
Book reader
Register marker
Picture painter
A good speller
Child lover
My teacher!

Luke Newman (7)
Wath Central Junior School

The Sea

See the dolphins splash
Hear the great roaring sea
Watch the sea whip up and down
Watch the waves
See the dolphins diving
Watch the tossing waves
See the sea crash at the rocks
The great sea roars.

Alex Levitt (7)
Wath Central Junior School

The Lovely Sea

Shells are nice and cold
The water is cold
I am splashing at my mum
I can see shells
Sharks are under the sea
The sand is boiling
The sea has got waves in it
The sea is warm.

Chloe Edwards (7)
Wath Central Junior School

The Splashing Sea

Babies paddling around.
Listen to the sea.
Children building sandcastles.
People splashing.
Shells coming to the shore.
People eating chips.
Watch the people snorkelling.
People packing.

Emily Fisher (7)
Wath Central Junior School

The Seaside

Building sandcastles
Hear the wind roar
Waves are coming close
Children swimming
Eating fish and chips
See the children snorkle
It's such a sunny day today
And yummy ice cream too.

Hannah Moore (8)
Wath Central Junior School

The Great Great Sea

People are sailing
People are searching
People like water
Ducks are in the water
Alex is surfing
Elliot is in the water
Seals on the rock.

Daniel Howell (8)
Wath Central Junior School

Metaphorical Me!

I am a speedy Komodo dragon.
My hands are burning fireballs.
My smile is a deadly warning.
My eyes are round cucumbers.
My voice is an exploding roar.
My laugh is a laugh of victory.
My hairs are shining daggers.
My feet are huge, pointy swords.
My heart is a juicy watermelon.

Jack Smith (10)
Wath Central Junior School

Bully In A Lorry

Candy to Conisborough
Iron to Ireland
Melons to Mexborough
Magnums to Manchester
Out of my way, faster, faster, faster
Out of my way, speed, speed, speed.
Out of my way, go, go, go.
Out of my way, quick, quick, quick.

Shay Murray (8)
Wath Central Junior School

Metaphorical Me!

I am an old, scruffy tramp sitting in the street,
My head is a titanic melon,
My neck is a tall, handsome lamppost,
My hair is scrumptious spaghetti,
My ears are rashes of greasy bacon,
My belly button is a mouldy, green pea,
My nose is a long, grey elephant's trunk,
My eyebrows are fuzzy caterpillars,
My arms are slithering snakes,
My eyes are twinkling stars in the moonlight,
My legs are fat, sizzling sausages,
My body is an immense tree trunk,
My voice is a contented playing harp.

Sarah Robertshaw (10)
Wath Central Junior School

Metaphorical Me!

I am a friendly pony, rolling freely in the golden sun,
My smile is a large dagger growing sharp and pointy,
My eyes are horseshoes shining brightly in the moonlight,
My hair is a group of woodland fairies granting me three wishes,
My feet are cuddly teddy bears, keeping me comfortable,
My hands are cheeky flamingos pecking at my toes,
My laugh is a group of playful apes swinging through the tall trees,
My nose is a squeaky toy making lots of tremendous noise,

That's metaphorical me!

Jade Newell (9)
Wath Central Junior School

Metaphorical Me!

I am a fox, who sneakily comes out at the strike of midnight.
My howl is a lion, roaring at you.
My nose is a giraffe's neck, never-ending.
My fur is a large red fluffy pillow, all full of lucky white feathers.
My smile is not a smile, it's a smirk.
My paws are massive JCB diggers, digging and leaving my mark.
My ears are pointed, sharp knives coming to chop you up.
My eyes are always open, like the world, *beware, beware!*

That's metaphorical me!

Dominic Jones (10)
Wath Central Junior School

The Prisoner

The shadows are phantoms swaying in this horrendous cell.
A mouldy scrap of food even too small for a mouse.
A frightening skeleton - he is my cell mate!
The guard looking at me like dirt - what an awful place.
All I did was take a loaf of bread, why am I here?
I am as lonely as an abandoned city.
I am as unwanted as a bug and the world is stamping on me.
I am as hungry as a lion with no food at all.

Get me out of here!

Emily Beaumont (10)
Wath Central Junior School

Little Miss Pear

Little Miss Pear
Sat on a chair
Eating her custard pie
Along came a tiger
And sat down beside her
And said, 'What's the problem?'

Freya Hewett (7)
Wath Central Junior School

The Prisoner

I am as petrified as a tiny fly
stuck to a spider's web.

My old empty bowl is a dry lagoon
begging for rain.

I am a famished lion
hunting in a desert wasteland.

I am as thin as a twig
on a scrawny tree.

I am almost identical to the skeleton
sitting in the corner.

I am a terrified mouse
waiting to be pounced on by an evil cat.

I am trapped by the rusty bloodstained shackles
scraping my skin like a sharp knife.

An ancient skeleton is sitting in the corner
promising my certain death.

Spindly spiders
scuttling across the damp, cold walls

And all I ever did
was steal a slice of stale bread!

Hollie Smith (9)
Wath Central Junior School

Little Miss Frog

Little Miss Frog
Sat on a log
Eating her Chinese takeaway
Along came an armadillo
Who came in a big limo
And fell right out of the window.

Rachael Duke (8)
Wath Central Junior School

Metaphorical Me!

I am a cheeky little monkey,
stealing someone's yellow banana.

My eyes are large blue bombs,
bombing my furious mum.

My hair is squirmy spaghetti,
cooking on the kitchen stove.

My ears are tiny white mice,
squeaking all day through.

My nose is a pink pig's snout,
sitting below my blue eyes.

My hands are 10 wriggly worms,
wriggling along the table,
trying to find my sharp pencil.

My arms are long springs
searching for scrummy food.

My eyebrows are long brown sticks,
trying to get some rest.

My smile is a brown branch off a tree,
curving with all its might.

My feet are little ducklings
swimming down the wavy stream.

That's metaphorical me!

Keeley Newell (9)
Wath Central Junior School

The Prisoner

Still, serious guards,
like statues being polished every day.

I am as angry as a petite spider,
dropping his midnight feast.

I am as terrified as a puny ant,
approaching a vast human body.

I am as hungry as a scruffy beggar,
waiting for some scraps of food
off the Lord's large table.

Sharp, pointing nails,
sticking out of the walls are certain death.

Scuttling, dirty rats,
racing like a cheetah
into each and every corner.

I am as lonely as the lifeless skeleton
hanging feet off ground before me.

Delicate, thin, spiders' webs, hanging over your bony head,
like the actual spider itself.

Lifeless, lonely skeleton, hung up
like a rabbit on a peg rotting away.

My only crime was to steal a loaf of bread
for my poor family.

My only escape is *death!*

Alice Woodcock (9)
Wath Central Junior School

Metaphorical Me!

I am a monster ripping up your home, doing a tornado spin,
My ears are gigantic elephants, stomping around,
My nose is a magpie's beak, stealing your riches,
My eyebrows are sharp daggers, stabbing vermin,
My smile is a lightning bolt, smashing antique glass,
My arms are jungle vines, winding round your body,
My hair is slimy serpents, slithering round my head,
My voice is an ear-splitting screech, scaring any animal.

That's metaphorical me!

Ruth Rocha Lawrence (10)
Wath Central Junior School

The Prisoner

Snowflake, delicate cobwebs
like a sticky net ready to grab me.

Rotten, crumbled skeleton
cracking every second making me jump.

Bloodthirsty, hungry rats
sniffing under my ankles.

Rusty, old shackles like rattlesnakes
sucking the life out of me.

I am a hungry beggar digging
through the Lord's scraps for food.

I am as angry as a lion
taken away from his family.

I am as lonely as that skeleton
staring at me in the dull darkness.

I am a bag of bones
waiting for hungry rats to eat me alive.

All I did was steal some bread
for my starving family and I get this!

Ashley Sturman (10)
Wath Central Junior School

Metaphorical Me

I am a seventy storey skyscraper, towering above the rest,
My arms are sharpened, chewed pencils, very, very thin.
My voice is an angry dog's bark, growling out words,
My ears are massive parachutes, flapping madly in the wind.
My feet are bustling car parks, moving me around.
My nose is a huge bridge, cars forever using me.
My eyes are heavy boulders, spying on everything.
My hair is a huge forest, swaying in the wind.
My laugh is a sonic sound wave smashing the air.
My hands are massive gorillas, grabbing at the world.
That's metaphorical me!

Thomas Andrews (10)
Wath Central Junior School

The Prisoner

Cracks in the gloomy walls where red ants
have made their nests,
I am as furious as a tiger cooped up in a tiny cage.
Cobwebs hanging off the grey moss-covered ceiling,
like a pit of doom.
I am as hungry as a begging bear,
waiting for my prey.
Vile disease carrying rats are just about
the only living things.
I am as thirsty as a plant that hasn't
been watered for a week,
Lifeless, lonely skeleton, sitting in the corner
with rats climbing through his dead ribcage.
I am as lonely as a child being separated
from its mum.
My only crime was to ask for a piece of bread
for my starving family.
My only way out is death!

Laura Lois Maskrey (10)
Wath Central Junior School

My Smartie

It's a round shape, like a ball,
Red as my school chair.
Smaller than a penny.

Hard as a rock,
Smooth as a table.
It wobbles from side to side.

Tickles my tongue,
Crunches on my teeth,
Yummy melting chocolate.

Aaron Gwatkin (9)
Wath Central Junior School

My Smartie

The shape is as round as a pebble,
The colour is as blue as the sea.
It is as shiny as a star.

It feels hard and smooth,
It is as solid as an ice cube,
It is as light as a gram.

The Smartie is as cold as the North Pole,
It is as soft as a ball of cotton wool.
The shell tastes brilliant.

Thomas Hammond (9)
Wath Central Junior School

My Simile Poem

A gorilla needs . . .
A head like a big, bouncing football,
A belly like a chubby muscular Sumo,
Feet like sharp knives,
Hands like a gripping giant.

It hits its chest and makes a noise,
It goes up a tree and goes to sleep.

Lewis Lowe (8)
Wath Central Junior School

My Smartie

It is as round as a pebble,
As yellow as the sun,
The Smartie is as bright as a sunflower,
But small, like a currant in a bun.

It is as hard as a mountain,
Smooth as a plate.

When I put it in my mouth,
It's just like eating sugar.
When I crunch, the taste changes,
Mmm! *Chocolate!*

Kimberley Frodsham (9)
Wath Central Junior School

Little Miss Dog

Little Miss Dog
Who sat on a log,
Eating her cottage pie
Along came a tiger
Who sat down beside her . . .
And then he fell off!

Shannon Skelton (7)
Wath Central Junior School

My Pets

In my bedroom, I keep . . .
Ten spotty dogs that go to sleep.
Nine butterflies that flutter around,
Eight little ducklings that walk funny.
Seven white-coloured cats that purr around you,
Six naughty monkeys that swing from the lights.
Five slow turtles that toddle around.
Four giddy puppies, that run about,
Three fat pigs that sleep and eat.
Two tadpoles that swim about,
One colourful parrot which copies what you say!

Amy White (8)
Wath Central Junior School

Happiness Is . . .

Happiness is at birthday parties, having fun,
Happiness is crazy fairgrounds.
Happiness is wedding days, brides and grooms.
Happiness is holidays, hot sun.
Happiness is Christmas Day, full of the joy.
Happiness is Mother's Day.
Happiness is going to friends' houses,
Happiness is Hallowe'en, scary times.
Happiness is Father's Day.
Happiness is Harvest Festival, food.

Sophie Kirkham (9)
Wath Central Junior School

Winter Poem

Patterned snowflakes falling down,
Fat filigree snowman standing still,
Pointed icicles hanging down,
Slippery ice on the frozen lake.
Biting air, swirling around,
Snowball fighting in a frosty garden.
Sparkling trees in a warm house.

Lucy Hardwick (8)
Wath Central Junior School

Worm Cinquain

The worm
slimy, sticky
slithering around leaves
wriggling in the dirty soil,
slimy.

Joshua Robinson & Megan Moffatt (9)
Wath Central Junior School

Happiness Is . . .

Happiness is Christmas morning,
Happiness is my birthday, hooray.
Happiness is a seven-week holiday,
Happiness is the thrill of cold, ice cream,
Happiness is McDonald's. Here we come!
Happiness is a shopping trip to Meadowhall.
Happiness is shooting down a waterslide.
Happiness is bathing in the sunshine,
Happiness is a holiday in Spain.
Happiness is your family's love.

Georgia Sanders (9)
Wath Central Junior School

My Smartie

The Smartie looks like the moon
The Smartie feels like a balloon.

The colour is grass-green
It feels cold as snow.

It is a smooth like a pebble,
The Smartie is hard.

It tastes scrumptious
I want all of them!

Casey Amanda Moule (9)
Wath Central Junior School

The Smartie

The Smartie is like a hard rock
This Smartie is like brown mud.
As smooth as a teddy's fur,
As crunchy as some crisps,
As small as a mouse.
The chocolate is creamy.

Kane Tasker (9)
Wath Central Junior School

Little Miss Mable

Little Miss Mable
Sat on a table
Eating her Irish stew
Along came a bee
And sat on her knee
So little Miss Mable ate up the bee
Along with her Irish stew!

Sophie Duggan (8)
Wath Central Junior School

All About Animals Alliteration

Pecking pelican
Nosy newts
Flying frogs
Foolish foxes
Funny fish
Shaking snakes
Dancing ducks
Cute cats
Chunky cats
Parading pigs
Trying tadpoles.

Lorna Joan Theaker (8)
Wath Central Junior School

Open The Door To Wildlife

Snapping, slithering snakes
Giggling gorillas
Hurrying horses
Kick-boxing kangaroo
Pinkie, pouncing pig.

Helena Leather (7)
Wath Central Junior School

All About Animals Alliteration

Hairy hiding hedgehog
Smelly silly sheep
Hot happy hamsters
Fierce flying fish
Diving dancing donkey
Wet wacky whale
Peeping purple puppy.

Joseph Elliss (7)
Wath Central Junior School

Wildlife

Whizzing round the place with wasps
Slivering, slimy snakes, all on the trees.
Big, bashing bulls running and banging
and wrecking.
Pinkie, pouncing pigs all wandering off
by themselves.
Mumbling monkeys all in the trees
Sleeping spiders in their homes.

Alexander Ng (8)
Wath Central Junior School

Cold Winter Poem

Icy lakes and biting air,
Snowballs down my neck.
Patterned snowflakes coming down.
Get a sledge and find a hill and go down
You go down, you go on the snow.
Or find some snow and build a snowman
And get some ice skates and go
Onto the icy lake and skate.

Julian Hermoso (9)
Wath Central Junior School

Bully In A Lorry

Strawberries to Swinton
Lollies to Leeds
Candy to Conisborough
Boots to Bulgaria
Out of my way! Go, go, go
Out of my way! Zoom, zoom, zoom
Out of my way! Hurry, hurry, hurry
Out of my way! Rush, rush, rush.

Madison Brown (8)
Wath Central Junior School

Happiness Is . . .

Happiness is when it's my birthday,
Happiness is when I wake up on Christmas morning,
Happiness is when I go on holiday,
Happiness is when I go dancing.
Happiness is when Haley does an impression of Elvis.
Happiness is when I go to my friend's house,
Happiness is when Megan laughs.
Happiness is when Sophie makes jokes,
Happiness is when I get medals.
Happiness is when I spend time with my family.

Rhianna Woodbridge (9)
Wath Central Junior School

The Harvest Mouse

The harvest mouse, it comes at night,
It's a harvest mouse.
It sings in the morning
It sleeps in the night.
It's a harvest mouse.

A harvest mouse runs in the rain,
It lays in the sun,
A harvest mouse.

A harvest mouse
I'll say goodnight
I'll say goodnight
Goodnight harvest mouse.

Shannon Louise Clayton (8)
Wath Central Junior School